Features from Life; Or, a Summer Visit, by the Author of George Bateman

by Elizabeth Blower

Address:
HardPress
8345 NW 66TH ST #2561
MIAMI FL 33166-2626
USA
Email: info@hardpress.net

FEATURES FROM LIFE;

OR,

A SUMMER VISIT.

PRICE SIX SHILLINGS SEWED.

SECOND EDITION.

FEATURES FROM LIFE;

OR,

A SUMMER VISIT.

BY THE AUTHOR OF

GEORGE BATEMAN, AND MARIA.

IN TWO VOLUMES.

VOL. I.

LONDON:
Printed for G. KEARSLEY, No. 46, Fleet Street.
M.DCC.LXXXVIII.

To Mrs. HASTINGS.

Madam,

WITH ſplendor and elegance of taſte we connect the idea of a lively imagination and a ſenſible heart; it is to theſe laſt qualities I apply when I ſolicit the honor of your patronage for theſe volumes. The weakneſſes and ſufferings of the leading characters they exhibit, appear to me to riſe naturally out of diſpoſitions replete with great virtues, and extreme tenderneſs; their misfortunes above all others the moſt likely to make a deep and eternal impreſſion on minds of

fine-

fine-wrought ſenſibility. If this little work ſhould meet with your approbation, I ſhall receive much pleaſure, and feel my ſelf-love greatly flattered.

I have the honor to be,

Madam,

Your moſt obedient

Humble ſervant,

The AUTHOR.

FEATURES FROM LIFE;

OR,

A SUMMER VISIT.

CHAP. I.

"HOW charmingly the thunder
"ſtorm has cleared the air and allayed
"the extreme heat; and ſee how beau-
"tifully the ſoft rays of the ſetting ſun
"gleam upon that little ſtatue!" ſaid
Matilda to Mr. Conway, as they entered
their elegant little ſaloon; "Do not
"direct my attention," returned he

"to that object, left it should tempt me
"to an act of imprudence. I had a let-
"ter to day from my friend Lewis, who
"informs me that the original, from
"which this cast was taken, is to be
"sold for only three hundred Guineas."
"Would that fate," cried Matilda,
"would exchange our hundreds for as
"many thousands a year, that it might
"not be imprudent in us to think the
"sum you mention a trifle."

"Heavens! my good girl, you do
"not think that I had a serious thought
"about the matter? I know it is a
"thing impracticable: I spoke but in
"jest: I hope, nay, I trust, I have en-
"tirely lost the desire of throwing away
"money in purchasing things of no
"real utility." "I wish," replied Matilda,
"with

with a look of animated ſweetneſs that went to the heart, " that it was in your " power to throw away money, as you " call it; for I am ſure there is no one " who would diſpenſe ſuperfluous caſh " more laudably, or after more elegant " acquiſitions."

" O! you ſimple girl, you muſt not " thus flatter ſuch a favourite propen- " ſity, unleſs you had the means of gra- " tifying it; for you may increaſe it to a " fault; and in our preſent circum- " ſtances you ſhould rather bid me to " conquer it."

" Alas!" ſaid Matilda, " it is not in " my power to reſerve"——

" I know it is not;" interrupted he, " but

“ do not, Matilda, think me ſo abſolute
“ a cognoſcenti as to be ſeriouſly hurt at
“ this affair. Could you believe, that
“ even if you had by an admirable œco-
“ nomy ſaved ſomething from the ſum
“ appropriated to family expences, that
“ I would accept it towards gratifying a
“ whim of mine ; Oh no.”

“ You interrupted me before you had
“ heard me out, Conway,” ſaid ſhe.
“ Now if you have ended, permit me to
“ finiſh what I begun to ſay.—I obſerv-
“ ed it was not in my power to reſerve,
“ and I was going to add the monoſyl-
“ lable *much*, if you had ſuffered me
“ to proceed. I have, however, at this
“ time, the ſum you want, and it is en-
“ tirely at your ſervice.”

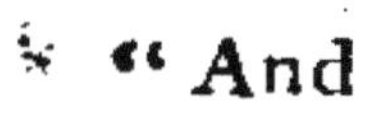
“ And

"And have you, indeed, done this; and "yet, without the appearance of re-"retrenching in the ſmalleſt article? I "did not think, when you ſeveral times "wanted me to hear about an overplus "of caſh in your hands, from the man-"ner in which our table is ſupplied, that "the charming miſtreſs who graced it "could have ſuch a ſum in bank."

"Yes, yes, I have; and I beg you to "take it without ſaying any thing more "on the ſubject."

"Oh! no, I cannot accept of it: "expend it yourſelf; you may find a "thouſand purpoſes for it: make an ad-"dition to your jewels; that is the only "ſort of finery you like."

"It is true," ſaid ſhe; "but be aſſur-
"ed I ſhall not purchaſe any with this
"ſum; ſo, I beg you will not think of
"refuſing to make uſe of it."

"I cannot help obſerving how
"ſtrangely it happens that you ſhould
"have laid up juſt the value of my lit-
"tle favourite. But was it really the
"three hundred Guineas?——within
"twenty or thirty pounds"——

"Extraordinary! but you ſurely
"could not think I would accept of it
"to ſpend myſelf, unleſs indeed you
"have as particular a wiſh to make the
"purchaſe as I have? I know no one
"who has a better taſte than yourſelf:
"but I do not recollect your ever ex-
"preſſing any ſtrong marks of admira-
"tion

" tion of this ſtatue. If you had any
" peculiar deſire yourſelf, the thing
" would be quite different."

" But, I have as great a wiſh to make
" the purchaſe as you have: and ſo be
" content on that head," ſaid Matilda,
ſtarting from her chair, and going towards the door--" I will fetch the notes
" for you this minute."

" But are you certain it is your own
" deſire?—"Yes, quite certain," ſaid
Matilda, going out at the door.

Charming woman! ſhe knew that to
preſerve a lively intereſt in the heart,
it is ſometimes neceſſary indulgently to
ſacrifice our own, perhaps, more pru-
dent inclinations to its innocent foibles.

The energy with which Matilda uttered the words "Yes, quite certain," ſet the mind of Conway at eaſe. He took a turn acroſs the room; and whilſt he admired anew the elegant object that had occaſioned the converſation, he fully reconciled himſelf to the indulgence of his own inclination, by flattering himſelf he was about to gratify that of another. We often ſee the beſt kind of people in the world practiſing this mode of agreeable deceit upon themſelves; what they like they are willing to believe, and they flatter themſelves, that a ready aſſent to their inclination does not ariſe merely from an obliging compliance with their taſte or pleaſurable purſuits, but from a ſimilar wiſh in the perſon who complies. Matilda returned in a few minutes with her writ-

ing

ing box in one hand, and the notes in the other. "Here are materials for "writing," ſaid ſhe; "I inſiſt that you "write immediately for the ſtatue to be "bought for you."

He ſmiled upon her with a look of enthuſiaſtic tenderneſs, and took the pen from her hand; at that moment there came in Frederick, his eldeſt boy, beautiful as an Angel, and holding in his hand a violin which (having always betrayed a partiality for muſical ſounds,) had been given to him for a plaything. The pen fell from the hands of Conway; he flung the notes into the lap of Matilda, caught the ſweet child in his arms; "take back your little treaſure, my lovely, my too-indulgent girl," ſaid he. "Why ſhould I expend money in

"purchafing a fculptured refemblance
"of the God, when I have a young
"Apollo glowing with life, health, and
"beauty; charming as the imagina-
"tion of the poet, or the hand of fculp-
"ture ever formed?"

The tender mother fmiled at the compliment to her little darling, whilft her heart exulted at this triumph of paternal affection, over an inclination which was juft going to lead to an improvident action. The little fellow felt the full force of the tender preffure which accompanied his father's compliment; he clung about his neck, and imprinted a thoufand affectionate kiffes on his cheek; but, in an inftant, fome new idea feized his volatile fancy; he eagerly flid from his embrace, and ran out of the room.

"See," ſaid Conway, with a ſmile of praiſeful love, "ſee, by what a mere "accident I was preſerved from liſten-"ing to your ſeductive wiles and acting "imprudently. Confeſs" continued he, with an air of ironical reproach, "that "you are——

"Well," cried ſhe, interrupting him, "perhaps it might not be quite right; "but I cannot bear that your generoſity, "oppoſed to my father's avarice, ſhould "abridge ſo many of your innocent "pleaſures." Conway could make no anſwer, but by holding her affectionately to his heart, whilſt the tears of grateful pleaſure ſtarted to his eyes, and added ſoftneſs to every line of a countenance where ſenſibility and dignity were blended.

Nature beheld the graceful weakneſ-ſes of theſe her favourite children through tears of delight: even Prudence, who had prepared a little reproof, now found her voice cheriſhed by riſing emotion, and hid her ſoftened features on the boſom of nature.

CHAP.

CHAP. II.

"MATILDA," exclaimed Conway, "I want words to expreſs my feel-
"ings, but my whole heart worſhips
"your virtues; yet, you muſt forgive
"me, when I confeſs that I do not even
"to others, ſo often as you deſerve them,
"make eulogiums on your actions. It
"ſometimes happens that in endeavour-
"ing to avoid a fault we run into the
"contrary extreme. I have ever had a
"peculiar diſguſt to a kind of falſe gra-
"titude which people often impoſe
"upon the world, and frequently, I be-
"lieve, upon themſelves for the true. It
"diſcovers itſelf in unſeaſonable and oſ-
"tentatious enumerations of the af-
"fection,

"fection, zeal, and services, of their
"friends. In many instances it is only
"a medium through which they seek
"to impress their auditors with high
"ideas of their own excellence, by
"displaying their power of attach-
"ing objects so worthy of estimation,
"as those are whom they take such ela-
"borate pains to praise."

"I entirely," said she, "enter into
"your sentiment; that passage in Pri-
"or's Henry and Emma has always
"appeared to me to possess a peculiar
"delicacy of thought when Emma
"exclaims to Henry,"

And whilst with secret joy and inward pride,
Which from the world my careful soul shall hide,
I see thee Lord and end of my desire,
Exalted high as virtue can require.

"That

"That paſſage of Prior has great
"beauty; nor do I recollect any au-
"thor who has expreſſed the thought
"with ſo much clearneſs and grace.
"How often, my Matilda, do I wiſh it
"was in my power to exalt you as high
"as your virtues deſerve. It is then on-
"ly that I repine at the narrowneſs of
"my fortunes—there is not any thing
"I would not do to add to your happi-
"neſs."

"Oh! do not wiſh me an increaſe of
"happineſs; but rather join with me in
"wiſhing that what I now enjoy may be
"continued to me. Conway, I ſome-
"times think we are too happy! ever
"ſince I have been capable of reflection,
"I have had an impreſſion on my mind,
"that when two perſons of ardent feel-
"ings

"ings and lively imaginations unite,
"some sad and weighty calamity gene-
"rally follows to give a balance to their
"lot, which would otherwise prepon-
"derate too much on the side of hap-
"piness, for beings born to look on
"this state of existence as only a pas-
"sage to another. Desire, preference,
"affection, are common to all; but, the
"electric fire of true passion, which now
"animates with delight, now desolates
"with despair the human soul, few
"hearts are formed to receive; it is a
"gift like true genius, or true beauty;
"but seldom bestowed; and, like those;
"when given, is oftener a source of mi-
"sery than of happiness."

The solemnity with which she spoke affected Conway at the moment; but he he aſſumed an air of ſprightlineſs, and replied: "Come, come, my dear girl, "we muſt not talk of felicity till we "grow unhappy: you muſt chaſe this "gloomy impreſſion from your mind: "I do not like your philoſophy: it is "too melancholy."

Juſt then their converſation was interrupted by the entrance of a ſervant who delivered a letter to Mr. Conway.

"From Sir Harry Gaythorne," cried Matilda, haſtily glancing her eyes over the ſuperſcription, "and con-"tains an account of his marriage I "dare ſay."

"It has moſt probably taken place by "this time," ſaid Conway, whilſt he broke

broke the ſeal, and immediately began to read. " This day has made me one of " the happieſt of the ſons of men: this " day has united me to one of the moſt " charming women in the world."

" Still yourſelf, Sir Harry," exclaimed Matilda in the midſt of joy; " you " have not loſt ſight of that ſentiment " of politeneſs which inſtructs us to a- " void wounding the feelings of others, " even in trifles as well as in more eſſen- " tial matters.

" Your expreſſions, One of the hap- " pieſt of the ſons of men! One of the " moſt charming women in the world! " prove you did not forget that you " were writing to a married friend. Sir " Harry's conduct forms one exception

" at

"at least, to the remark of a spirited "and elegant writer, "that it is the "characteristic of felicity to be unfeel-"ing."

"When I write," said Conway, "I "will pen your eulogium for my friend; "—but now hear the request he makes to "you.—"It is the earnest request of La-"day Gaythorne and myself, that you "and Mrs. Conway will spend the first "winter with us in town: and we will "have the happiness of spending part "of the summer with you in the "country. Lady Gaythorne has form-"ed the most exalted ideas of the ex-"cellence of Mrs. Conway's character "from the description of your friend, "and is impatient to become acquainted "with so charming a model of every "domestic

" domeſtic virtue."—There! ſurely you
" cannot reſiſt this? Come what an-
" ſwer ſhall I write to him?"

" I ſincerely hope nothing will hap-
" pen to prevent your having the plea-
" ſure of congratulating your friend in
" perſon on his marriage."---"How eva-
" ſive a reply is that!" ſaid Conway: " but
" I confeſs, I expected it; the little air
" of diſcontent that clouded your fea-
" tures when I read the invitation, told
" me you did not wiſh to go as plainly
" as if you had uttered the words; and
" were I not certain that your diſincli-
" nation ſprung from the beſt motive in
" the world, your care of your chil-
" dren, I ſhould be ex[illegible] hurt at
" it. That motive, howev[illegible] ay be
" obviated, as you have a fr[illegible]nd in
" whom

"whom you can repoſe ſo full a confi-
"dence."

"It is true, I could; if you wiſh it,
"I will leave my children to the care of
"Mrs. Bates; but I confeſs I ſhould not
"be ſo happy as if I had them under
"my eye. Diſſipation under ſuch cir-
"cumſtances would be doubly irkſome;
"for even when I trod the giddy round
"of pleaſure, before I had taken on me
"the important cares of a married life,
"the ſolidity of my education left a
"ſenſation on my mind, that often re-
"proached me for ſo unprofitably ſpend-
"ing my time; and often amid the
"glitter of faſhionable amuſements, I
"have beheld the venerable form of my
"admirable Mentor, ſiſter Frances,
"beckon me to retreat, reminding me
"of

" of the ſtudious, the elegant hours I
" ſpent in the convent of——"

" My dear girl," ſaid Conway, " I
" ſhall preſently begin to fancy you poſſeſs
" the extraordinary powers aſcribed to
" the highland ſeers. You propheſied
" once before, and now you talk of the
" gift of the ſecond ſight. But however,
" I may be convinced of the goodneſs
" of your intentions in declining this
" viſit, I am afraid Sir Harry and Lady
" Gaythorne will take it unkindly. You
" ſhould remember, that a virtue carried
" to an exces, degenerateſs into a fault."

" But ſurely," ſaid Matilda, " 'tis my
" duty to"——"Yet," interrupted Conway,
" we ſhould not let the practice of one
" virtue ſuperſede the performance of
" another.

"another. I think you would be acting
"meritoriously in visiting this young
"woman: your example would be of
"great advantage to her. The change
"in her situation is a very great one:
"she is but just released from the prac-
"tice of a plan of rigid œconomy adopt-
"ed by her mother, to enable them to
"make a genteel appearance from an
"income otherwise insufficient to sup-
"port them in that respectable rank of
"life in which they were born. By her
"marriage with Sir Harry she is raised
"to rank and affluence: the youthful
"mind bounding from restraint, too
"often takes an irregular direction. Be
"it yours at least to endeavour to coun-
"teract the effects of those glaring
"blandishments by which fashion and
"extravagance so often seduce a young
"mind,

" mind, suddenly raised to grandeur,
" into the vortex of folly and dissipation.
" Go, my Matilda; let her see how
" gracefully the sober tints of domestic
" virtue may be blended with the light
" and animated colouring of polished
" wit and fashionable elegance."

Matilda returned a bow and a smile for this compliment. But ah! how different from the grimace of ceremony, or the exulting smile of gratified vanity. It was the sweet smile of affectionate gratitude, and the lovely animation of conscious worth. The flexibility of Matilda's nature would have tempted her to have given up the point rather than to have contended with Conway; but she thought herself in the right, and strove against the impulse of

 her

her feelings, which in this caſe ſhe deemed a weakneſs, as ſtrongly as many a turbulent ſpirited lady has been obliged to combat with an intemperate tongue, in order to maintain her reputation for high breeding. But, to return to the converſation; "you are far more partial to my little merits than they deserve," ſaid Matilda: "I think that
" a poſitive duty is not to be neglected
" in order to attempt to perform a good
" action, which however beneficial in
" its conſequences, we are uncertain of
" achieving. I know that I can be of
" ſervice to my children by ſtaying at
" home; and I am ſure if Lady Gaythorne need a pattern of right conduct, ſhe will find examples even in
" the great world, more likely to awaken her attention, and influence her

" actions, than so imperfect a one as
" mine could do."

" Do not exert yourself to argue far-
" ther on the subject Matilda," said
Conway with an air of reserve; " you
" know I never yet suffered you to com-
" ply with a request of mine when I
" could not convince you that it was
" right. Say no more about it; I have
" done with it;" and so saying, he took
up his hat and quitted the room. The
tone of his voice was not in the least
raised above his ordinary speech; and
his guestures were perfectly calm; but
there was a little haughtiness in the
elevation of his neck which Matilda had
often remarked as majestic dignity it-
self, but which she now viewed with

 concern,

concern, as it convinced her he was ſtill diſpleaſed.

Matilda thought it beſt not to ſay any thing more on the ſubject that evening, but to let the matter reſt till the little diſpleaſure Conway ſeemed to feel had ſubſided. She accordingly, when he returned into the houſe, began with the moſt pleaſant caſt of countenance ſhe could aſſume, a different converſation; and he, probably tired of their late ſubject, though not reſolved to give up the point, was not at all diſpleaſed with a ceſſation of their contention for the preſent.

CHAP. III.

THE next morning, immediately after breakfaſt, Conway went out of the parlour, and paſſing into the garden, ſaid to a ſervant that he met, " If a perſon " of the name of Barton, from Green- " wood Farm, ſhould call, let him be " ſent to me—I am going to walk in the " ſhrubbery."—Matilda, in a medita- ting humour, ſat down to her needle- work ;—ſhe wiſhed ſhe had not ſaid ſo much the evening before; or that her rhetoric had been more prevalent. Thus reflecting, ſhe ſat for about a quar- ter of an hour, when determining, either by more perſuaſive arguments to endea- vour to bring him to her opinion, or to yield

yield gracefully to his, as ſhe ſaw occaſion, ſhe put aſide her work and walked into the garden. She had reached that part of the ſhrubbery where Conway was; the ſpreading branches of a laurel tree ſcreened her from his ſight, when a man, whom ſhe knew not, approached the ſpot:—Matilda then recollected the orders which he had given on quitting the room; and ſuppoſing the ſtranger came on buſineſs, ſhe would not interrupt them, therefore, ſtill ſhaded from their ſight, ſhe ſeated herſelf upon a garden chair to wait till the perſon ſhould depart. Through the leafy coverture, however, ſhe could plainly diſcern their geſtures; even the expreſſion of their countenances.—The man a plain, well-looking farmer, approached with ſomewhat of that timid, irreſolute air which poverty, ſuperadded to affliction, generally gives.—Conway returned his bow with great affability.

"I ſent for you, Mr. Barton," ſaid Conway, "in order to"—"I apprehend "ſo, Sir," ſaid the man, anſwering to what he imagined the other was about to ſay;—"I am very ſorry that I have "not been able to be as regular in pay-"ing my rent as uſual, and as I am "ſure I hoped always to have done, "but I had a bad getting in laſt harveſt, "for my wheat was mildewed before "I could carry it off the field, ſo it ſold "at a great loſs, Sir; and as my turnips "did not do well neither, my cattle "have been ſadly pinched, and I have "loſt a good many. But my crop on "the ground, thank God, looks pro-

"miſing,

" miſing, and I will threſh out enough
" as ſoon as ever I get it into the barn,
" to pay what I ſhould have paid at
" Midſummer; ſo I hope, Sir."

" Say no more by way of apology,
" Mr. Barton," ſaid Conway, interrupting him in his turn, " as you have been
" accuſtomed to make your payments
" regularly, I ſhould not have ſent to
" you on that account; I had another
" reaſon for requeſting you to call upon
" me.—I want to know whether your
" father did not poſſeſs an eſtate called
" Elm-wood Farm, in the county of
" ——; can you recollect ever having
" heard him mention any thing concerning its falling into the poſſeſſion of
" Mr. Johnſtone?"

" I was too young," replied Barton, " when my father died to have been told " the particulars, but I remember to " have heard him ſay that eſtate belonged " once to my grandfather; and that was " he himſelf a man poſſeſſed of property " ſufficient to enter into a lawſuit, with- " out fear of hurting his family, ſhould " he loſe his cauſe, he would try to get " it out of the hands of an attorney, " who had unjuſtly got it into his poſ- " ſeſſion."

" To this Mr. Johnſtone," replied Conway, " I was diſtantly related by " my mother's ſide; and, at his death, " this eſtate devolved to me as his heir " at law, but on looking over ſome pa- " pers, I find many reaſons to believe " if you were to commence a ſuit

" againſt

" against me, you might make out a
" better title to it than I can."

A ray of hope and pleasurable surprize animated the poor man's aspect for a moment, but quickly disappeared.—
" Alas! Sir," said he, " do not talk of
" law;—I have no money to go to law
" with."—" I have no doubt" said Conway, " of your gaining your cause;—
" and as I believe you to be an honest
" man, I will lend you money, and
" you may repay me as soon as you have
" it in your power."

An offer made with so much apparent sincerity, so unexpected, and so uncommon, almost overwhelmed the poor man, whose health had been greatly impaired by distress of mind. Matilda saw his change of countenance, and an expreſ-ſion of compaſſionate concern diſcovered her to Conway. Barton, recovering himſelf, attempted to expreſs his gratitude.

"I only render you juſtice, Mr. Bar-"ton," ſaid Conway, waving his thanks."—"Think over this matter in "your own mind and if you will let "me ſee you to-morrow morning at ten "o'clock, we will then talk farther on "the ſubject, and I will give you the "beſt advice I can how you ought to "proceed.

"I would thank you, Sir," ſaid Barton, "if I could, but I have not words "—I am all amazement.—What, Sir! "not only tell a poor needy man where

"he

" he may find a treaſure, but put a ſpade
" in his hands to dig it up, to your own
" detriment!—Good God! I did not
" think there had been ſuch goodneſs,
" ſuch nobleneſs in the world as this!"
He bowed reſpectfully and retired.

"Alas!" ſaid Conway, turning to Matilda, " depraved indeed muſt the
" age be, when even to an honeſt man
" an act of juſtice, in the leaſt degree
" out of the common road, appears
" like an act of generoſity."

"It is true," ſaid Matilda, taking his hand with an air of affectionate reverence, " your voluntary avowal to the
" man, that you have reaſon to think
" yourſelf not the lawful owner of the
" eſtate, is only acting with ſtrict inte-

"grity; but your offer to fupply him
"with money, certainly entitles you to
"the praife due to a generous action."

"I do not know," replied Conway,
"whether it would not have been a
"want of charity not to have lent him
"money.—I do him a material fervice,
"and I am in no danger of hurting my-
"felf."

"But why did you conceal from me
"your intention?" faid Matilda; "if
"I have not your ftrength of under-
"ftanding, I have, I truft, a kindred
"rectitude of principle."

"I did not doubt, Matilda, your
"ready concurrence in my intention,
"and I was about to communicate it to
"you

" you yesterday, but the arrival of Sir
" Harry Gaythorne's letter, and our
" subsequent conversation, prevented
" me."

"But why, my dear Conway, should
" this poor man, who is now in distress,
" wait the tardy process of the law, if
" you are convinced he has a right to
" to the estate."

" It appears to me that he has," said
Conway; " but I would have it proved
" so to others.—You know, my good
" Matilda, that even should your father
" leave us all that we have a right to ex-
" pect, which, considering his disposi-
" tion, is not probable; the fortunes of
" our children will not be large; and
" as the comforts of life are few—the
" sorrows

" ſorrows many, we have no right to
" leſſen, in the ſmalleſt degree, any
" one's portion of the gifts of for-
" tune; even though we took only from
" his abundance to give to one whoſe
" allotment was too ſcanty for his ne-
" ceſſities: for it is probable, how par-
" tial ſoever the diſtribution may ap-
" pear, that this unequal poſſeſſion of
" one good, may be counterbalanced by
" the total deprivation of ſome other.
" Therefore I would not willingly be
" reproached, nor would I have to re-
" proach myſelf with having, through
" what may be called a romantic idea of
" juſtice, given away ever ſo ſmall a
" portion of our children's birth-right.

" A child of your's reproach you?"
ſaid Matilda, kindling at the thought,
" it

" it can never happen.—The child who " does not glory in ſuch a father, ſhould " it poſſeſs the faſcinating powers of a " ſyren, I would tear from my heart."

"I thank you, my good girl;—I " thank you," returned Conway, much affected; " but had we not better walk " towards the houſe?"

They turned to go in. In their walk Conway revived the ſubject of their friend's marriage; but took care by no direct word whatever, to requeſt that ſhe would go to town. The affectionate reverence with which the incident juſt recorded, had filled Matilda's breaſt, robbed her of the power of contending, but ſhe wiſhed him to give her an opportunity of ſhewing him ſhe yielded to his ſolicitations; and though he did not again, in direct terms, repeat his requeſt, ſhe could plainly enough diſcover it was the wiſh of his heart that ſhe ſhould comply with it, by his uſing, in the courſe of their converſation, the oblique expreſſion "*as you have determined not to go to town.*"

Matilda, deſpairing of a more open utterance of his deſire, ſtopped, turned round, and putting her hand in his, anſwered by a look,—"I have *not* ſo determined; lead me where you will."

"You will go then!" ſaid Conway. "—Do I read right?"

"I purpoſe it," returned Matilda.

"How

" How much may be faid" cried Conway, " without the articulation of " a word !"

" Yes," replied Matilda, " it has of- " ten ftruck me, that the language of " the tongue was only defigned by na- " ture for the negociation of bufinefs ; " for things affectionate, foothing, or " witty, may be faid by the eyes much " more forcibly."

" One might indeed juftly infer fo, " Matilda," faid Conway, fmiling at this little fally, " had nature given to " every one eyes as expreffive as yours."

CHAP. IV.

CONWAY had not finiſhed ſpeaking two minutes, before a ſervant approached, and told them their little Charles, mentioned before, was taken ill. Matilda's countenance inſtantly evinced the truth of Conway's late aſſertion; the ſtrongeſt expreſſion of maternal anxiety overſpread her features, whilſt ſhe flew to the Houſe without uttering a ſingle word. She was too much alarmed for inquiry. Conway followed with feelings not leſs acute. They beheld their child extended on the knees of a female attendant; the beautiful bloom of his complexion was changed to a livid blackneſs. His limbs were diſtorted by convulſive

vulſive ſpaſms; every vein was ſwelled beyond its natural ſize, and his features were made hideous by contorſion. Such was now that lovely infant, whom ſo recently his fond father had held to his heart, exultingly exclaiming, that his little frame, glowing with life, health, and beauty, exhibited a more ſtriking reſemblance of an infant Apollo than the imagination of the poet, or the hand of the ſculptor ever formed!—Matilda, ſpringing haſtily forward, took the child and laid it on her lap; and whilſt her head bent over it, the big drops of ſorrow rolled from her cheek on its livid forehead. "Go inſtantly," ſaid Conway to one of the women, "tell "Philip to fetch Dr. J——."

His mandate was inſtantly obeyed.

As

As Conway held the liltle convulſed hand of the poor infant in his, his heart ſmote him with having too importunately ſolicited the tender, anxious mother to quit her children, In the deep anguiſh of her heart, Matilda was ready to exclaim, " Ah, ſee what " conſtant care, what unwearied atten- " tion theſe little beings demand!"— But ſhe checked herſelf on caſting her eyes on Conway's face, which appeared the picture of grief:—" No, not even " in the extremity of my own woe, will " I add to his affliction!"

Dr. J—— arrived as ſpeedily as the diſtance would admit, but only arrived to diſpel all hopes of the child's recovery, who, according to his prediction, expired before another day dawned.

The

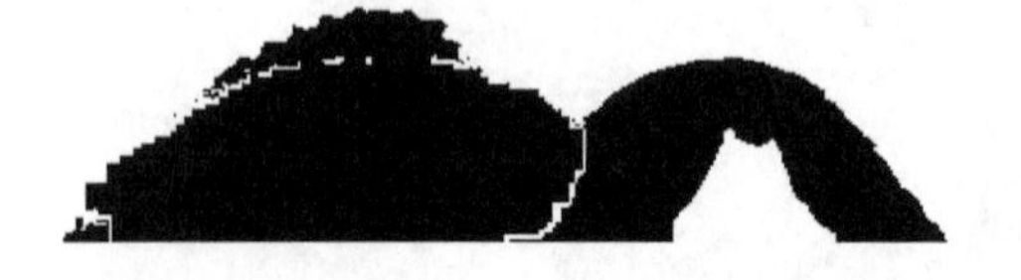

The parent's heart, formed in nature's roughest mold, and the soul of exquisite sensibility, will here mutually sympathize; for such is the selfishness of human nature, that even the greedy, unfeeling heir, whose heart bounded at hearing of his father's death;—who saw, without a sigh, a venerable and affectionate mother, brought by his vice and folly with sorrow to the grave;—who can behold a tender wife, the victim of his cruelty, expiring by slow but sure degrees, without remorse, has yet wept in bitter anguish; has melted even to infantine weakness at losing a child, a living resemblance of himself.

CHAP. V.

THIS calamitous incident retarded as will naturally be ſuppoſed, their journey till winter had nearly given place to ſpring. Matilda would far rather ſtill have indulged her melancholly in the country; but Conway, who thought the change of objects might give a new turn to her ſpirits, united his own to the preſſing intreaties of Sir Harry and Lady G——, that ſhe would ſpend a few weeks in Groſvenor-Square, as they had promiſed to ſpend part of the ſummer with Mr. and Mrs. Conway in the country. The news-papers had already announced to them that Lady Gaythorne had depoſed the ſovereign of former winters,

winters, and now reigned ſole empreſs of the wide and brilliant provinces of taſte; that the dreſs in which ſhe was preſented at court, had been a model for the faſhionable world ever ſince; that Gaythorne hats, Gaythorne caps, and Gaythorne trimmings, were the high rage of the day. Her name never appeared in the public prints, but preceded by the epithets of lovely, elegant, enchanting, &c. &c.

Theſe circumſtances joined to the high opinion they had of Sir Harry's taſte and judgement, led them to conclude that Lady Gaythorne was at leaſt, a pretty or a fine woman. As to her being a perfect beauty, they made due allowances fot the exaggeration of fame, who ſeldom diſcriminates ſufficiently amidſt

amidſt the ſplendor of high rank, and the trappings of fantaſtic finery, to make a correct portrait. But as ſome years had elapſed ſince the Conways had mixed much in the gay world, their eyes, long accuſtomed to the natural beauty and ſimple neatneſs of the provincial ladies, could ſee no charms in the gaudy ſubſtitutes of art, and conſequently the perſon and attire of Lady Gaythorne had few attractions in their ſight. But as I hope to have the honour of being read by ſome of thoſe whoſe habits of thinking were early formed in the great world, and never afterwards ſpoiled by ſecluſion from it, I ſhall for their amuſement embelliſh my work with as accurate a likeneſs of the lady now in queſtion as my pencil is capable of delineating.

I The

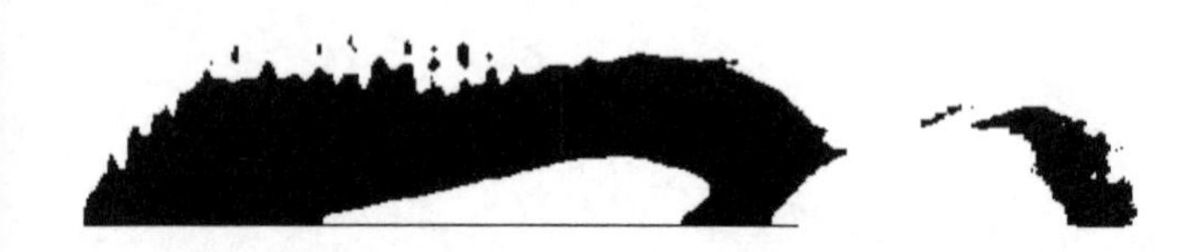

The precise age of Lady Gaythorne, I find impossible to ascertain: several persons who were intimate with her parents at the time of her birth, confidently declared she had seen her six and twentieth birth day before the period at which these memoirs commence. But this evidence there is, I grant, some cause to doubt, as the person most nearly concerned in the affair, Lady Gaythorne herself, always averred she was no more than eighteen; and we are credibly informed, as a corroborative circumstance, that her Ladyship's mother when speaking of her, even after her marriage, constantly used the epithet of young girl, or young thing. But as I pique myself on a strict impartiality, which is certainly one of the most material characteristics of a good

 historian,

historian, I cannot refrain from inserting a thought which has this instant struck me, though it may in some degree weaken the force of the last fact.

The learned and ingenious author of the essay on antient virgins having gallantly declared it his opinion, that the æra of old maidhood does not commence till the age of forty-three: I think, and Lady Gaythorne's mother it is probable had the same idea, that according to this calculation the period of girlhood may be fairly extended beyond the age of twenty-six; and that of boyhood too. Nor do I doubt having on my side in support of this sentiment, those two able advocates, the witty, the eloquent Mr. Fox, and his brilliant friend Mr. Sheridan: ground-

ing my reliance on their having ſo often in their animated and claſſical orations ſtiled our wiſe young miniſter a boy, after, as I apprehend, he had paſſed that age.

But to the portrait.

Lady Gaythorne was tall, and thin even to leanneſs; her features were regular, but not one of them had the leaſt pretenſions to be called handſome, (except her eyes which were well ſhaped and of a finé blue,) nor was the want of beauty made up by the charms of an engaging aſpect: an inſolent pride being the prevailing expreſſion of her countenance, except when to ſerve any particular purpoſe ſhe cloathed it in the wily ſmiles of allurement or diſſimulation.

By leading the faſhions however, ſhe found out a remedy for almoſt every defect: the hollowneſs of her cheeks, and the ſallowneſs of her complexion, ſhe rectified by a liberal uſe of the beſt fard and rouge: and ſhe continued to take from the length of her viſage by having her hair dreſſed full round her face and low down upon her forehead, ſo as to hide a conſiderable part of it.

The meagerneſs of her neck was concealed by an artful arrangement of flowing curls; and the deficiency of a riſing cheſt, aptly apologiſed for by an immenſe protuberance of gauze, lace, or muſlin, ſupported by wire, catgut,

&c. &c. The extraordinary length and flatneſs of her arms from the ſhoulder to the elbow, ſhe concealed by a large full ſleeve tied with bunches of ribbands; and to increaſe the beauty of that part of her arm, which the cuſtom of this country authoriſes every lady to ſhew undraped, a pair of black velvet braceiets encircled her wriſts, which by making them look ſmaller gave ſomewhat more the appearance of a gradual ſwell to the upper part of her arm. Her feet which nature had a little unkindly formed rather large and flat, were according to the French faſhion pinched into a pair of ſhoes, the ſoles of which ſcarcely exceeded the breadth of a half crown piece; but by this ardent compreſſure the inſtep was forced to a greater height, and the defect of nature by that means happily atoned for.

But, there is yet another exquisite stroke of her ladyship's art that remains to be recorded, and which I beg pardon for not inserting in its relative situation, The skilful statuary by a judicious use of the chissel, can, when he has formed the shoulders of a female figure too high, easily reduce them to the line of beauty : but though a woman of fashion when blest with a happy genius, can as (I think I have shown) do much to increase the elegance of her own form, of a reduction similiar to that in the sculptor's power, there is I believe, at present no precedent.

It

It only remained therefore for lady Gaythorne to revive the Elizabeth Ruff, and introduce the immenſe handkerchief; and thus from a refinement of art, if ſhe could not give her own form the ſymmetry ſhe deſired, ſhe amply compenſated for the want of it in herſelf, by introducing a faſhion which rendered it of no effect in others. For let a ſtatue of Therſites, or Æſop, and the Venus de Medicis, be habited in the Gaythorne mode, and they would appear equally graceful. Having reſided from her childhood at St. Omers, ſhe had acquired that free familiar air which diſtinguiſhes the French provincial ladies; but without their wit and engaging vivacity. She ſpoke the Engliſh tongue fluently, though with a foreign accent: this laſt circumſtance was however, by no means a disadvantage to her; it gave a certain childishness to her articulation which affected the ear like the tones of simplicity; and which co-operating with a soft flexible voice, served in some degree to meliorate the strong lines of art which appeared in her person and manners.

CHAP.

CHAP. VI.

IT was between the hours of ſeven and eight in the evening when Conway and Matilda arrived at the elegant manſion of Sir Harry Gaythorne. At the door of the apartment to which they were ſhewn, they were met by Sir Harry, who with a countenance beaming with pleaſure, led them to Lady Gaythorne.

"Our friends, Mr. and Mrs. Con-"way."

Lady Gaythorne uttering every expreſſion the vocabulary of good breeding furniſhes for ſuch occaſions, after having returned the bows of Mr. Conway, took the hand of Matilda and led her to a ſopha at the upper end of the room. Sir Harry and Conway again ſeized the hands of each other, repeating expreſſions of joy at this meeting, with a warmth that delighted Matilda, who inſtantly turned her eyes towards Lady Gaythorne, expecting to find her employed, and equally charmed with herſelf in contemplating the looks of friendly affection which animated the countenances of both. But her Ladyſhip was much more importantly engaged than in tracing the lines which the gentle and generous affections of the ſoul impreſs on the aſpect; for the ends depending from a knot of ribband on one of her ſleeves were not of an equal length, and ſhe was buſied in adjuſting

this

this part of her drapery. Having compleated it, ſhe turnd to Mrs. Conway and told her, "ſhe had ſuffered a great "deal from having been ſo long depriv-"ed of the happineſs of ſeeing her "and Mr. Conway; and thanked them "both for the honour and happineſs "they gave her by their viſit."

Mr. and Mrs. Conway were making the politeſt return to this compliment, when a thundering footman's rap ſhook the houſe with a violence that muſt totally have deranged her ladyſhip's nerves, had it proceeded from any other cauſe than that of announcing viſitors. Of this we have not the leaſt doubt, having been credibly informed, that though ſhe never diſcovered the ſmalleſt emotion, but ſat with the utmoſt fortitude during the laft-mentioned noife. The heavy mechanical double knock of the poftman never failed making her ftart, complain of her nerves, and declare that the found went quite through her brain, and put her whole frame in agitation for a quarter of an hour afterwards.

Sir Harry continued talking with his friend till the found of feet and the ruftling of filks on the ftaircafe caufed him to exclaim with furprife, turning to her Ladyfhip—"Your orders have "been neglected!—I requefted this even-"ing we might be denied to other vifitors; "thinking after fo long a journey it "would be more agreeable to Mr. and "Mrs. Conway."—There was no opportunity for any anfwer from Lady Gaythorne;

thorne; but a look of displeasure which she had hardly time to chase from her features when the servant entered and announced—" Lady Witlington, and " Mrs. Neville." Lady Gaythorne having paid her compliments with great respect to the former, vouchsafed a nod and courtesy to the latter. She placed Lady Witlington on the sopha beside Mrs. Conway, and Mrs. Neville sunk into the first unoccupied chair on which she cast her eye.

" Did your Ladyship see Mara's " entrée at the Opera?"

" Yes, and was enchanted! What a " voice! What brilliant execution!— " But I own I was vexed to hear her " receive so much applause: the insolent

" lent caprice of her late conduct ought
" to have been punifhed by marks of ne-
" glect and contempt."

" Why wifh it fhould be fo?" faid Sir
Harry. " I fear that the public in general
" is too apt to delight in humbling the
" fpirits of perfons of great fuperiority
" of talents, who from want of fortune
" are dependant on it for fupport and
" protection, whilft the pride and arro-
" gance of the rich and great pafs fre-
" quently unnoticed, always unpunifhed."

" Oh! becaufe we have it not in our
" power to punifh them," replied Lady
Gaythorne.

" Pardon me; we have it always in
" our power to fhew our difapprobation
" of

" of their conduct in the way just men
" tioned, by marks of neglect and con-
" tempt. How wide is the difference!
" If in this age of frivolity and dissipa-
" tion, a man or woman of fashion con-
" descends to cultivate the smallest ta-
" lent for arts, science, or literature,
" their performances are extolled with
" rapture; candid critism is precluded,
" and the arbitraty umpire, fashion,
" stamps their value. They meet, per-
" haps, with some few instances of per-
" sonal envy; but this is amply made
" amends for, by the unmixed applause
" they receive from the many. On the
" contrary, what is his lot who is ne-
" cessitated to depend for the means of
" existence on even the sublimest efforts
" of Heaven-born genius? Why the
" supercilious, affected disregard of many

"ny who underſtanding his excellence, "want the ſoul to ſpread the worth "they love; and the ignorant commen- "taries, and even the inſolent diſdain "of thoſe who can neither underſtand "nor judge. It ſhould ſeem, that we "feel humbled to receive pleaſure from "our inferiors in birth and fortune, and "take theſe methods of revenging our- "ſelves for the ſuperiority nature has "given them over us."

A little beam of pleaſure lighted the penſive features of Mrs. Neville while he ſpoke. "Moſt truly ſaid, Sir Harry," cried Lady Witlington; "you have "ſpoken what my ſoul feels. It is a "view of human nature, that almoſt "makes one aſhamed of being of the

the

" the same species with individuals
" capable of sentiments so illiberal."

Lady Gaythorne either did not, or pretended not to pay the least attention to what Sir Harry had been saying; and when Lady Witlington had ended, she turned to her with an air, whether real or fictious, that implied she had been reflecting on a very important subject. " Pray," said she, " did your " Ladyship obseve Mrs. W——'s hat, " the night of Dido: was it steel or dia- " mond that glittered so violently at a " distance?"

Sir Harry appeared mortified to the quick; his eye brows grew more elevated at her affected inattention to the conversation which had passed, and the hue

hue of refentment fhot fwiftly into his cheeks; but making an effort to fuppress the emotion of anger, it died away, and his features fettled into the languid look of difappointed hope.

Lady Witlington replied, "fhe really "could not determine;" and juft then Mr. Needham was announced.

CHAP.

CHAP. VII.

IN this gentleman's character there was fomething very fingular; it was a character little underftood. He paffed for a cynical obferver and commentator on the follies of mankind; whilft in reality, he made his way in the world by a confummate knowledge in the art of flattery. His father, who was for many years a merchant of great eminence, foon after young Needham had compleated his ftudies at the Univerfity, died infolvent. Whilft he was in the agonies of furprife and affliction at this melancholy change in his affairs, a young gentleman who had lately fucceeded to his paternal inheritance, and into

into whoſe friendſhip he had inſinuated himſelf at College, gave him an aſſylum in his houſe, and ſettled upon him an annuity of a hundred pounds a year. Here he was introduced upon a footing of equality to the beſt company.

Happening, however, to give offence to the lady his friend, a few years after married, he was genteelly diſmiſſed from the houſe, and though he ſtill continued to viſit there, it was plain he was not welcomed as an intimate friend. Accuſtomed to the indolent ſoftneſſes, and the brilliant amuſements of high life, he knew not how to relinquiſh them, and he revolved a thouſand ſchemes in his head for enabling a man poſſeſſed of a bare hundred pounds a-year, to ſhare in the voluptuous indulgences, the expenſive penfive pleafures of the affluent. He faw the thing done every day by thofe who had the faculty of applying themfelves with addrefs to the weakneffes, the vices, the caprices, of mankind.—And what he had feen of life had fhewn to him, that the readieft way to the goal he aimed at was by the road of fome fpecies of adulation. He faw the beaten road of indifcriminating flattery fo thronged, that he feared he fhould be often joftled in his paffage, and, perhaps, at laft, totally overfet by fome of thofe who poffeffed more of the graces of manner than himfelf. He refolved, therefore, to ftrike out a path for himfelf, which yet fhould eventually lead him to the fame point. He determined to become a general cenfor, and a partial flatterer;—

but

but imagine not, reader, his encomiums were confined to the rich and powerful: he found it his advantage sometimes to bestow them on persons not distinguished by these advantages; and in this he was judicious, for it had to slight observers the appearance of disinterestness, which, aided by the austerity with which he inveighed against the vices of the great world, made his praises more ardently coveted; and more highly estimated when obtained.

He had fathomed the depth of Lady Gaythorne's understanding; he knew the extent of Sir Harry's fortune, and played his cards accordingly. He had a sort of sarcastic wit, which entertained; and as it is not difficult to make our conversation admired on an ill-natured subject

ſubject *without* this ingredient, yet when it is intermixed, it grounds a reputation for the talent of ſhining in converſation, that nothing can ſhake. For though ſome, through good-nature, and others from a dread of being laſhed in the ſame way, feel uneaſy ſenſations; yet the far greater number of the auditors will be thorough admirers; for there is but a ſmall part of the world who ſee their own characters clearly enough to think themſelves objects for ſatiric animadverſion; and of thoſe who on ſuch occaſions feel for others, *very ſmall indeed* is the number. Even thoſe who, from a timidity of diſpoſition, fear a ſatiriſt, will court him for the ſame reaſons,—from a dread, and a knowledge of his malignity; as the ſimple Indians worſhip

worship the Devil, to court him not to four their palm wine.

Sir Harry Gaythorne, on the entrance of Mr. Needham, had crossed over to that side of the room on which Mrs. Neville sat, and began a conversation with her, by saying, "What do you "think, Mrs. Neville, of the new dance, "Il Convito di Pietro?"

"I saw great part of it with admira-"tion," returned she.

"I thought it a subject worthy the "contemplation, and likely to strike "the imagination of an historical paint-"er, which made me mention it."

"Oh,

" Oh, good Heavens !" returned ſhe, " there is in the attitudes, the expreſſion " of Lepicq, the boldneſs, the terrible " graces of Angelo, the abaſhed, the " ſelf-reproaching humility ;—the re-" morſe-ſtruck airs, which Guido knew " to give in a few of his pieces, beyond " every other maſter. I declare I know " no modern profeſſor of any one of " the imitative arts, who could depict " the paſſions with greater force or juſt-" neſs than Lepicq."

" Little Neville" ſaid Needham, with a patronizing and ſagacious air, " you " ſpeak very well as an artiſt, but " though as ſuch you may be allowed " to contemplate Il Convito di Pietro " with delight, the tongue and the pen " of the moraliſt ſhould ſtigmatiſe it as

" an exhibition that marks the profliga-
" cy of the age in colours the moſt glar-
" ing. And I have no doubt, if repre-
" ſentations of this kind continue to
" be encouraged, but the Chriſtian
" idea of future puniſhments will con-
" vey as little horror as the heathen no-
" tion of Tartarus ; and the records
" of ſcripture be as familiarly ran-
" ſacked for materials for dramatic
" compoſition, as have been the pages
" of mythological ſtory. Nor ſhould I,
" I confeſs, be ſurprized to ſee a panto-
" mime announced, taken from ſome
" paſſage in holy writ. The Tempta-
" tion, for inſtance,—and the Aſcent of
" Satan, bearing to the pinnacle of a
" high rock the Saviour of the World,
" immortaliſe ſome Harlequin of the
" preſent day."

" Good

" Good God! you are too ſevere, " ſurely, Mr. Needham," ſaid Lady Witlington; whilſt looks of ſurprize and momentary awe paſſed over the countenances of all but Lady Gaythorne, who with an air of indifference replied, " I " hate pantomimes; I never ſtay to ſee " them; the boxes are always empty be- " fore they begin."—" True," replied Sir Harry; " and I am inclined to " think, bad as the age is, repreſenta- " tions of that kind muſt for ſome time " longer be confined to dances at the " Opera; for I much queſtion whether, " conſidering the higher claſs of people " go out before the pantomime begins, " there would at preſent be found a par- " ty ſtrong enough to ſupport them."

"Oh, Sir," returned Needham, "but ſpectacles of that kind would, I "have no doubt, inſpire a rage for the "tricks of Harlequin, and rivet our "people of rank as firmly to their ſeats "as ever did the graces of Veſtris, or the "majeſty of Simonet; for an appear- "ance of irreligion can give conſe- "quence to the meaneſt objects, and "throw an air of faſhion over the vul- "gareſt amuſements."

"I ſhould be afraid," ſaid Mr. Con- "way, ſmiling, "that the taſte of the "age would be much againſt the revi- "val of any thing like the long-explod- "ed farces, called the Myſteries and "Moralities—But if the idea of them "were ſo far revived as to make the "Devil a character in modern farces, it "would

" would have one good effect,—it would
" reconcile us, in ſome degree, to the
" monſtrous plots and unnatural inci-
" dents, ſo much the dramatic faſhion
" of the preſent day; as, in thoſe an-
" cient pieces, the Devil was invariably
" the *plotter of all the miſchief.*"—Farther converſation on the ſubject was prevented by Sir Harry's aſking Mrs. Neville, if ſhe ſhould exhibit at the Royal
Academy any of her paintings this year?

" Only one piece," ſhe returned;—
" the ſubject is Minerva conducting a
" young pupil to the Temple of Sci-
" ence:—it was begun at the requeſt of
" Lady Witlington, and the principal
" figure is a portrait of her ladſhip."

"Had Mrs. Neville's talents been in "the Hogarthian ſtile," ſaid Needham, ſpeaking to Sir Harry in a key loud enough for thoſe who ſat next him to hear, and yet ſo whiſpered as to give the party in queſtion ſome colour for ſeeming not to hear; "and ſhe had deſigned "to repreſent a wrinkled hag, conduct-"ing a young pupil to a modern Tem-"ple of Venus, I ſhould have com-"mended her choice of a ſitter."

Mrs. Neville changed colour, and the reſt who heard him looked abſolutely terrified. But Lady Witlington, with an admirable preſence of mind, pretended to be too deeply engaged in converſation with Lady Gaythorne to apprehend they were talking of her. The attention Needham had paid to Mrs.

Neville,

Neville, had given that lady ſome ſort of conſequence with Lady Gaythorne, for ſhe had looked once or twice towards her; and that without any haughtineſs in her aſpect. Lady Witlington had, perhaps, perceived this, and thought it the favourable moment to propoſe the thing for which ſhe had introduced her protégée to Lady Gaythorne;—for ſhe ſaid, " Mrs. Neville would think her-
" ſelf much honoured if your Ladyſhip
" would ſit to her pencil for ſome hiſto-
" rical figure, as it will undoubtedly be
" a means of bringing her talents into
" notice."

" Is portrait painting her forte?"

" She has great excellence in that
" way."

“ And you tell me ſhe has pieces
“ every year in the Exhibition ?—Well,
“ I will call to-morrow morning and ſee
“ her pictures ;—but does your Lady-
“ ſhip think there will be time to finiſh
“ a picture of me before the Exhibition
“ opens ?—for that is a material point
“ with me ; as I aſſure you my ſole mo-
“ tive in having one done is to ſerve
“ your friend.—Three of the firſt artiſts
“ have my portrait in hand at this
“ time.”

Having accompliſhed, by this ſacrifice to Lady Gaythorne's vanity, the
point ſhe aimed at, Lady Witlington
told Mrs. Neville the honour Lady
Gaythorne deſigned her ;—and after the
cuſtomary forms had paſſed, Lady Witlington and Mrs. Neville withdrew.—

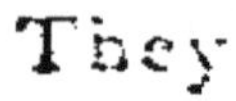

They

They had ſcarcely left the room, when Needham launched into animadverſions on the ſervice it would be of to the fame of the paintreſs, to delineate a figure ſo diſtinguiſhed for beauty as Lady Gaythorne's.

The former part of Needham's converſation, though ſome of his ideas had a little ſtartled her, had rather tended to prejudice Mrs. Conway in his favour; ſhe thought many of his ſtrictures well meant and ſtriking, but his coarſe manner of ſpeaking of Lady Witlington had diſguſted her a good deal; for from the intereſt ſhe ſeemed to take in the ſucceſs of Mrs, Neville's talents ſhe was inclined to think well of her head and heart: and therefore as ſhe ever made it a point to ſpeak all ſhe could in favour of thoſe ſhe heard depreciated, ſhe took occaſion, when her ladyſhip had diſappeared, to commend her zeal in the cauſe of the perſon whoſe abilities ſhe patroniſed.

"All a farce, madam?" returned Needham, haſtily;—"I have had op-"portunities of knowing Lady Wit-"lington's character well, and ſhe is "ſenſible of it, which was the reaſon "ſhe would not ſeem to hear what I "ſaid.—Towards this very woman, "whom ſhe pretends to patronize, I "know ſhe has acted baſely.—The fact "is this:—Lady Witlington, ever ſince "a certain affair has been talked of, "finding herſelf but coldly received by "many of her friends, and the circle of "her acquaintance likely to diminiſh,

"prudently

" prudently bethought of ſetting up
" herſelf as a patroneſs of the profeſſors
" of arts and ſcience; and by the libe-
" rality with which ſhe ſpends her mo-
" ney, and the *eclat* of a title, ſhe con-
" trives to bring about her a number of
" that claſs of people;—by this means
" ſhe has collected in her train of viſit-
" ing acquaintance, perhaps, upon the
" whole, characters more reſpectable
" (though not ſo brilliant with reſpect
" to exterior ſplendour) than thoſe ſhe
" formerly aſſociated with; for, with
" the hope of meeting perſons with ta-
" lents congenial to their own, many
" people of rank who are diſtinguiſhed
" for worth and a love of elegant art
" and liberal ſcience, honour her par-
" ties with their preſence.—And, by de-
" grees, I dare ſay ſhe will again be re-

" ceived by every defcription of perfons
" who figure in the world of fafhion.—
" But to the immediate fubject.—Mrs.
" Neville was the daughter of one of
" Lady Witlington's tenants, a reputa-
" ble farmer in —— fhire:—the girl
" had been educated at a country board-
" ing fchool, where fhe had been taught
" to draw by an indifferent mafter who
" attended the boarders. Some fketches
" fhe had made were accidentally fhewn
" to Lady Witlington, when fhe was in
" the country, and an *amateur* of fafhion
" who was then on a vifit to her lady-
" fhip, pronouncing them above medi-
" ocrity, fhe thought that a favourable
" opportunity prefented itfelf for diftin-
" guifhing her love of art, and her philan-
" thropic difpofition at the fame time, fhe
" accordingly fent for the young woman,
" took

" took her into her houſe, and furniſhed
" her with proper maſters to finiſh her
" education ; particularly attending to
" that art ſhe had ſhewn the dawn of abi-
" lities to excel in. Here ſhe continued
" ſtudiouſly endeavouring to improve
" by the aſſiſtance offered, and gave no
" cauſe of diſguſt, till a young man of
" immenſe fortune, the nephew of Lady
" Witlington, and to whom Lord Wit-
" lington had been guardian, by coming
" frequently to the houſe, appeared to
" have conceived the ſtrongeſt admira-
" tion of Miſs Markland's charms,
" worth, and talents ; and as her lady-
" ſhip knew him to be amiable, and of
" that ſpirit which minds of her lady-
" ſhip's caſt are pleaſed to ſtile roman-
" tically generous, ſhe feared he would
" offer honourable addreſſes to her pro-

" tegée

" tegée,—a circumſtance ſhe could not
" think of with patience, as his eſtate,
" in caſe of Mr. Manſel's dying with-
" out an heir, Lord Witlington had
" left to her ladyſhip.—She remon-
" ſtrated with him in the ſtrongeſt terms
" againſt the diſhonour he was about to
" bring upon their family, by deſcend-
" ing to a plebian alliance. She even
" added hints, reflecting on the morals
" of Miſs Markland; but Mr. Manſel ſaw
" the deſign ſhe aimed at, and they had
" no other effect on his mind than to
" irritate him to ſay, he thought a wo-
" man of worth, however lowly born,
" did more honour to a family than one
" of illuſtrious birth, whoſe actions
" were ignoble. This ſtroke, which
" ſhe could not but perceive was meant
" for herſelf, fired Lady Witlington with

" ſo

" ſo ſtrong a reſentment, that ſhe deter-
" mined, at all events, to gratify her
" pride, avarice, and revenge by fruſtra-
" ting their union; and ſhe inſtantly ſet
" every engine at work to bring about
" her purpoſe. She knew Mr. Manſel
" was going out of town the next day,
" and ſhe had drawn from his converſa-
" tion of this day that he had not yet
" made a direct offer of his hand and
" fortune to Miſs Markland, and ſhe
" contrived to engage her ſo that he
" could have no opportunity of ſpeak-
" to her alone that day.

" As ſoon as he was gone ſhe entered
" upon the ſubject ſhe had been for ſome
" days thinking of.

" 'My dear Markland,' ſaid her lady-

" ſhip with a tone of kindneſs, ' I have
" long been thinking of ſome way of
" eſtabliſhing you in life, that may be a
" certain reſource when I ſhall be no
" more ; a period, which, conſidering
" my ill ſtate of health, may not be far
" diſtant.—I have ſomething to propoſe
" to you, which I hope will be approved
" by you.'

" The poor girl, with tears of grati-
" tude thanked her ladyſhip for her kind
" concern, and ſaid ſhe was ſure ſhe could
" ſuggeſt nothing but what was for her
" beſt intereſt. Lady Witlington then
" ſaid ſhe had heard of a perſon who was
" remarkably clever at embroidery, who
" wiſhed to find a partner who had a
" turn for flower painting—Now as this
" appears to me, added her ladyſhip,
" not

"not an ineligible plan, if you approve
"it, I will advance the few hundred
"pounds required, and you ſhall imme-
"diately enter into buſineſs, and I can
"almoſt inſure you ſucceſs, for I will
"recommend you to all my friends.—
"The words 'enter into buſineſs,' ſtruck
"Miſs Markland to the heart; and
"whilſt Lady Witlington was deliver-
"ing this ſpeech ſhe felt as if undergo-
"ing a ſudden metamorphoſis;—to be
"thus in a moment degraded from an
"hiſtorical painter to a little pattern-
"drawer for an embroiderer, was too
"much!—ſhe could not articulate a
"ſyllable for ſome minutes; at laſt ſhe
"burſt into tears.—'What have you to
"object, Miſs Markland,' ſaid Lady
"Witlington,—'this is the firſt time
"I ever perceived in you ſymptoms of
"ingratitude.'

"Oh

" 'Oh, madam!' returned ſhe, en-
" deavouring to ſtifle her tears, ' I am
" not, I will not be ungrateful—but I
" had flattered myſelf—I had hoped—'

" 'With what had you flattered
" yourſelf—what had you hoped, Miſs
" Markland?'

" 'I had hoped, encouraged by your
" praiſes, and thoſe of the friends you
" procured me, that I ſhould have been
" able to provide for myſelf in time by
" the practice of a more elevated talent.'

" 'But you know, my child,' return-
" ed her ladyſhip, appearing to ſoften a
" little, ' the ſucceſs of exertions of that
" nature is very uncertain; and many
" years muſt elapſe before great even
" artiſts

" artiſts can extract a ſupport from
" their labours—they muſt wait till
" time and the voice of the public have
" given a ſanction to their abilities :—
" beſides, it really takes a courſe of
" years to acquire excellence ſufficient
" to gain the applauſe of unprejudiced
" judges, and I could willingly ſee you
" ſettled in ſome certain way of provid-
" ing for yourſelf; for the delicacy of
" my conſtitution renders the tenure of
" my life very precarious.—I aſſure you
" when I was laſt ill I thought much
" about you; and I reſolved, if I reco-
" vered, to ſee you ſpeedily fixed in
" ſome way of life—for it is dreadful to
" think to what a fine young woman
" like you might be ſubjected, without
" the means of providing for herſelf."

" Miſs

"Miſs Markland, who had all the "real modeſty of true genius, with a "ſingular meekneſs of ſpirit, was much "ſtruck by the words 'unprejudiced "judges;'—ſhe began to fear leſt the "applauſe ſhe bad received might have "been given in compliment to the par- "tiality Lady Witlington was ſuppoſed "to have for her; and that ſhe had "over-rated her own talents. She cal- "led to mind,—or rather what had been "ſaid recalled to her mind, that her "birth entitled her to no higher ſitua- "tion than that her patroneſs was pro- "poſing to place her in; and reflections "like theſe ſerved a little to ſilence "thoſe feelings of diſguſt which roſe at "the firſt hearing Lady Witlington's "propoſition; yet, though ſhe ſubmit- "ted without murmuring, ſhe could

"not

" not without lamenting. She recollect-
" ed it was not only a change of ſitua-
" tion, but a change of ſociety, ſhe was
" about to experience ;—but looking on
" theſe feelings as the ſuggeſtions of a
" ſpirit revolting at the diſpenſations of
" Providence, ſhe ſtrove to ſubdue
" them, and with the beſt grace ſhe
" could command, expreſſed her ſub-
" miſſion to what her ladyſhip thought
" for her beſt intereſt. They went that
" day and inquired the particulars they
" wiſhed to know of the perſon in queſ-
" tion ; and it now only remained to pay
" the compliment to her father of ſub-
" mitting the ſcheme to his opinion.—
" This was immediately given in fa-
" vour of her ladyſhip's plan.

" The

" The day was fixed for her going;
" —ſhe went—with what ſentiments
" may eaſily be conceived.

" When Mr. Manſel returned from
" the country he inquired where Miſs
" Markland was?—he was told ' gone
" into the country.—' He aſked to be
" informed where, but this was deciſive-
" ly denied by Lady Witlington.—He
" then declared to her ladyſhip he would
" write to Mr. Markland to inquire the
" reſidence of his daughter;—but the
" very moment he had quitted the houſe,
" Lady Witlington ſat down and wrote to
" Mr. Markland, to warn him againſt
" diſcovering to Mr. *Manſel* the place
" where ſhe had fixed his daughter;
" telling him his deſigns reſpecting his
" daughter were not of a right nature,
" and

" and that it was fearing they might
" prove fatal to her honour, that ſhe
" had removed her from her houſe,
" and wiſhed to conceal her from Mr.
" Manſel. The good man, in conſe-
" quence of this letter, reſolutely re-
" fuſed him any information. Theſe
" obſtacles had the contrary effect from
" what her ladyſhip wiſhed; they only
" heightened the paſſion ſhe hoped
" they would ſubdue.—He employed
" intreaties, expoſtulations, tears, to
" draw from Lady Witlington the place
" of Miſs Markland's abode, but ſhe
" was inexorable. Fearing, however,
" that a paſſion ſo violent, acting on a
" mind ardent by nature, would in time,
" in ſpite of all her machinations,
" achieve what it aſpired to enthuſiaſti-
" cally, ſhe planned a ſcheme, vile in
" its

" its projection, and fatal in its execu
" tion; engaging in it one whom ſhe
" knew had an inclination for the perſon
" of Miſs Markland—this was a Mr. Ne-
" ville, a painter, who had been former-
" ly one of her ladyſhip's favourites in the
" line of gallantry, and whoſe abilities
" as an artiſt, by her indefatigable ex-
" ertions, ſhe had brought into notice;
" ſhe told him if he would gain the hand
" of Miſs Markland ſhe would preſent
" him with a thouſand pounds. As he
" was at this time much preſſed by im-
" portunate creditors, and really was
" charmed with the perſon of the young
" lady, he reſolved to leave no attempt
" untried to bring about an event, in all
" reſpects to him deſirable. By Lady
" Witlington's advice he took apart-
" ments at the houſe where ſhe had
" placed

" placed Miſs Markland ; here he paid
" her the moſt unremitted attentions,
" and uſed all the rhetoric he was maſter
" of to conciliate her affections, but in
" vain ; ſhe was reſolute in her refuſal.
" Determined, at all events, to effect
" the purpoſe he had in view, he put in
" practice a ſtratagem which had at firſt
" been mentioned to him by her lady-
" ſhip as their *dernier reſort.* As he
" boarded in the family, he had eaſily
" an opportunity of infuſing into ſome-
" thing ſhe drank at ſupper, a ſleeping
" potion. The ſomniferous draught
" ſoon operated ; ſhe withdrew. He ſtaid
" with the other lady till ſhe retired for
" the night, and then found the cham-
" ber of the unhappy Miſs Markland, on
" whom the ſoporific liquor had had its
" natural effects. The morning came—
 " abandoned

" abandoned to deſpair, ſhe attempted
" to deſtroy herſelf—he prevented her :
" ſhe flung herſelf into a coach, and was
" driven to the houſe of her falſe friend;
" he followed her as faſt as poſſible ;
" he was there almoſt as ſoon as herſelf.
" She had not had time to articulate a
" word when he appeared—ſighs, tears,
" and convulſive groans alone had told
" her ladyſhip her diabolical plan had
" had its wiſhed-for conſequence.

" 'Approach not, thou monſter !'—
" cried Miſs Markland ; but finding he
" ſtill advanced, ſhe was flying out of
" the room.

" 'For heaven's ſake !—ſay one of
" you what is the meaning of all this !'
" cried

" cried Lady Witlington, with an air
" of the moſt finiſhed hypocriſy.'

" 'Oh, detain me not another mo-
" ment in his preſence!' cried Miſs
" Markland, 'or ſure I am I ſhall do
" ſome deed of deſperation.'—He bar-
" red her paſſage—he knelt at her feet
" —pleaded the violence of his paſſion,
" which nothing could ſubdue—ſwore
" that he had been inſtigated to the ac-
" tion he had committed by the hope
" that ſhe would marry him; and with
" every mark of well-acted paſſion in-
" treated her inſtantly to promiſe him
" that happineſs.

" She rejected him with the bittereſt
" reproaches—he implored the media-
" tion of Lady Witlington. Enough

" had now fallen from them to permit
" her ladyſhip with *propriety* to *ſeem* to
" underſtand ſomewhat of the cauſe of
" this ſcene ;—ſhe burſt forth into
" the loudeſt and moſt opprobrious in-
" vectives againſt Neville, and ſeemed
" ſtrongly to abet Miſs Markland in her
" refuſal of his offer. When her lady-
" ſhip had played this part as long as
" ſhe thought neceſſary, ſhe, after hav-
" ing at his earneſt entreaty, ſpoken with
" him ſome minutes alone, ſhe return-
" ed to Miſs Markland, and apparently
" melted by his ſupplications and peni-
" tence, even ſolicited her to accept his
" hand. She painted to her, that if any
" thing of what had paſſed ſhould tranſ-
" pire, the world, which always ranks
" itſelf on the male ſide, would never
" receive her among the number of the
" innocent ;

" innocent; and that ſhould her father
" hear any thing to her diſhonour, it
" would bring his reverend hairs with
" ſorrow to the grave. By arguments
" and ſuggeſtions like theſe, ſhe ſtrove
" to perſuade her that nothing remained
" to preſerve her honour but to give
" him her hand. Miſs Markland was
" long inexorable; but Lady Witling-
" ton, at laſt, deploring her obſtinacy
" and blindneſs to her own intereſt, ſaid
" that if ſhe perſiſted in ſentiments ſo
" injudicious, ſhe muſt withdraw her
" countenance and protection.

" The thought of being left to the
" world unpatroniſed, with perhaps a
" tarniſhed character; the diſtreſs of her
" parents, roſe to her mind: bewildered
" between the ſupplications of the one,

 " and

" and the arguments of the other, ſhe
" was at length led to the altar. Their
" marriage was announced in the papers;
" young Manſel ſaw it, and madneſs was
" the conſequence. His friends were
" obliged to put him under the care of a
" phyſician, eminent for his ſkill in treat-
" ing perſons afflicted in that way. He
" was removed to the Doctor's houſe a
" few miles from town.—Here Mrs. Ne-
" ville viſited, and happening to be walk-
" ing in the garden, one of the ladies of
" the family requeſted her to ſit down in
" a little arbour to ſing to them: ſhe be-
" gan. It chanced that Mr. Manſel, who
" was at that time in a melancholy and
" quiet ſtate, had been ſuffered to ramble
" about the garden. The ſound of a
" voice ſo well remembered drew him
" to the place; the ladies who were
" with

" with her perceived him approach, but
" Mrs. Neville did not. He continued
" fixed to the ſpot as if beholding a vi-
" ſion that he feared would the next mo-
" ment diſappear, till ſhe had ended
" her ſong; when darting eagerly towards
" her, he exclaimed with looks of the
" moſt enthuſiaſtic delight.— Have I at
" length found her?—Yes! it is ſhe,
" and I am bleſt for ever. He ſeemed
" to have entirely loſt all ideas of her
" marriage, and entreated her in the moſt
" paſſionate terms to conſent to unite her
" fate with his. She could make no re-
" ply; the agitation of her mind was
" only expreſſed by her countenance.
" She at length diſengaged herſelf, and
" haſtened from him, accompanied by
" the other ladies. He ſtrove to overtake
" her, and ran wildly from thoſe who

" attempted to detain him. But, a lucid
" moment being lent him, the recollection
" of her marriage flashed upon his memo-
" ry.—She is married! exclaimed he,
" stopping his course, and flinging himself
" on the ground, and then wandering
" again: Ah! she can never return: Lady
" Witlington will never let her return.
" And this thought again drove him to
" that deplorable state of phrenzy, from
" which he had so recently emerged.

" The good little woman," continued Needham, " has an infinity of fortitude;
" and, I believe, she is looking towards
" another world, for that happiness she
" can never expect in this."

" Lady Witlington still with the utmost
" appearance of anxiety, exerts herself

" to

" to ſerve Neville and his wife, and in " this ſhe acts with judgement: ſhe thinks " her continued intercourſe with them, " and her zeal in behalf of their ſucceſs " in life, will appear as evidence againſt " the truth of reports, which in ſpite of " all her caution have circulated to her " diſadvantage."

The whole company were much affected by the particulars they had heard; and Sir Harry, looking at Lady Gaythorne, ſaid; " how were you " introduced to Lady Witlington?"

" I met her Ladyſhip at Mrs. Cole- " ville's aſſembly, and I thought I " could be guilty of no impropriety " in making the acquaintance, as I ſaw " her at the houſe of ſo reſpectable a " a lady."

"Yes," ſaid Needham, "ſhe often "receives a card when Mrs. Coleville "has a public night; for that lady, it "is well known, piques herſelf more on "the fullneſs of her rooms on her aſ-"ſembly nights, than on her beſt vir-"tue. But Lady Witlington is never "admitted to her private parties, nor "let in when ſhe calls in a morning; "and her viſits are always returned by "a card, and Mrs. Coleville's chariot, "which ſhe contrives to ſend, when it "has ſet her down at ſome houſe in "her Ladyſhip's neighbourhood."

Needham ſoon after roſe and departed.

The moment he was gone, Sir Harry riſing haſtily, rung the bell; when a ſervant appeared, "how came it," ſaid

he,

lie, "that you let in company when "Lady Gaythorne desired no one might "be admitted."

"My Lady Sir, told me she would "be at home to every one; and I re-"ceived no orders since to the con-"trary."

"You will remember now then," said he, "that your Lady desires that "no one may be admitted." When the servant had disappeared,

"If you recollect, I requested that "you would be denied to every one "but our expected friends—I thought, "after a long journey, a family party "would be more agreeable to them than "accidental visitors or promiscuous

 "company.

" company. I am ſure, to me, an even-
" ing ſpent in their ſociety, unmixed
" with any other, has always afforded
" the higheſt, trueſt, enjoyment."

An effort to mantain her character for good breeding, baniſhed a miſty cloud from her Ladyſhip's brow, and with a blandiſhing ſmile, drawing back her head, and juſt lifting up and ſhewing the palms of her elegant ſpread hands, with a look of the moſt pretty girliſh wonder and recollection, ſhe ſaid; "Oh! I beg your pardon, but
" I entirely forgot your requeſt. I am
" obliged to you for reminding me:
" we ſhould have loſt an infinity of
" pleaſure by admitting other com-
" pany." This ſhe ſaid, but not from her heart: however, the ſmile, the

playful,

playful, yet ſelf-reproaching, action entirely ſubdued Sir Harry's diſpleaſure. Such charms has even the ſemblance of good humour and ingenuouſneſs; and the reſt of the evening paſſed away in converſation on the part of Sir Harry and his gueſts, affectionate, lively, pleaſant, and profitable.

CHAP.

CHAP. VII.

WHEN they were alone, Matilda remarked that Conway appeared thoughtful; and, ſhe was not at a loſs in gueſſing the ſubject of his reflections. The truth is, Conway experienced, at that moment, that ſenſation of pain which a delicate mind feels, to acknowledge, even to itſelf, that the judgement or conduct of a beloved friend has been erroneous: and, though he much wiſhed to relieve his mind by converſing with Matilda, he could ſcarcely bring himſelf to confeſs, even to this ſecond ſelf, that he thought with a degree of contempt of the woman his friend had made choice of—and, Matilda gueſſing by

by her own thoughts, and his ſilence, what was paſſing in his mind, avoided mentioniong Lady Gaythorne. At laſt, however, he ſaid, " Tell me, Matilda,
" what you think of Lady Gaythorne.
" I know you will give me your true
" ſentiments, for I have ever found
" you ſuperior to that little weakneſs
" which hangs about many good wo-
" men, who, fearing the imputation
" of a tendency to detraction, run into
" a contrary extreme; and, by ſpeaking
" well of all, forfeit juſtly their claim
" to the praiſe of giving the palm to
" merit alone. — Truth thinks not of
" the opinion of others, but when
" called upon, boldly delivers its own."
" So, now, Matilda, I have furniſhed you
" with an unanſwerable reaſon for ſpeak-
" ing your real ſentiments.—" I confeſs
" to

" to you," ſaid Matilda, "ſhe is a very
" different woman from what I always
" thought would have been the choice
" of Sir Harry Gaythorne; and, that
" ſhe is one with whom I would never
" form an intimate acquaintance."

" I ſhould have known," ſaid Conway, " that the chords of her heart
" did not vibrate in uniſon with yours,
" had I only heard her ſing. She has
" the advantage of a good voice, ſhe
" executes in a good ſtile, with neatneſs, and even a degree of brilliancy,
" but ſtill there is a ſomething wanting."

" There is wanting that expreſſion,
" which gives a ſoul to harmony itſelf,
" and for which nothing can compen-

" ſate!

" ſate! When I underſtood that the
" mother of Lady Gaythorne was
" the widow of an Engliſh Officer of
" a noble family, who had retired to
" St. Omer's, in order to bring up her
" daughter, and live in a ſuperior
" manner on her ſmall income, than
" ſhe could in England, I had imagin-
" ed my friend's wife a well-bred,
" well-informed woman, unaccuſtomed
" to the frivolous purſuits of diſſipa-
" tion, and untinctured by thé flippant
" airs that diſtinguiſh her followers.
" My opinion of her mental qualities
" had been regulated by my know-
" ledge of Sir Harry's general good
" taſte, his ſuperior underſtanding,
" his worth, and elegance of ſenti-
" ment. I begin, now, to give credit
" to what Wilmot, who, you know,
" viſited

" visited them at St. Omers, said of
" them, though at the time I attend-
" ed not to his observations, knowing
" that his strictures on the female part
" of his acquaintance, are generally
" more remarkable for sarcasm, than
" candour and justice. But, I am of
" opinion he spoke the truth when he
" said, 'He had looked behind the
" cards and perceived how the game
" was likely to terminate.' He ob-
" served that the mother and daughter
" played into each other's hands; the
" former was anxious to make it ap-
" pear, that three men of superior
" rank and fortune, who visited at the
" house, were desirous of obtaining
" the hand of her daughter: to these,
" she paid the most assiduous attention,
" whilst Sir Harry was present; taking
" no

"no more notice of him, than the
"rules of politeneſs and hoſpitality
"demanded. The daughter, on the
"contrary, appeared totally inſen-
"ſible to their attentions, (which,
"in fact, were no more than every
"man of gallantry thinks himſelf un-
"der an indiſpenſable neceſſity to pay
"to a fine woman) whilſt even a glance,
"a ſmile of approbation, from Sir
"Harry, ſeemed to give her extreme
"ſatisfaction.—If ſhe ſung a plaintive
"air, the tenderneſs it breathed was
"all directed to him; and, if ſhe
"danced, ſhe looked at no one but
"him for admiration and applauſe.
"Theſe *ſeeming* indications of a paſſion,
"to which he could not be blind,
"joined to the conduct of her mother,
"who acted the part of a woman, in-
"vincibly

" vincibly determined to dispose of her
" child to the highest bidder; without
" consulting her inclination, flattered
" that degree of self love which every
" man possesses, and gave birth to a
" better sentiment, that of pity for
" her situation. He thought the at-
" tachment she displayed, disinterested;
" for, her mother's artful conversation
" and deportment had persuaded him
" that she might match higher, if for-
" tune was her only object. He wish-
" ed her happiness, he was anxiously
" interested in what concerned her;
" from some motive or other he felt
" himself drawn to seek her society.—
" From these sensations, as he had
" never loved, he fancied that he now
" loved; he acted accordingly; he
" married."—" And, I fear Wilmot's

" words

"words are already verified," That "the ſeeds of frivolity which the con-"duct and leſſons of her mother, had "ſo thickly ſown in her boſom, when "warmed by the ſunſhine of proſpe-"rity would ſoon ſpring up and over-"ſhadow for ever, the happineſs of "our friend."

Matilda only anſwered by a look, that expreſſed her pity for the diſappointment of one whom her mind had pictured ſo amiable as it had Sir Harry; and the converſation, for that time ended.

CHAP.

CHAP. VIII.

THEY were at the Opera the next evening, and from thence went to Ranelagh. At their entrance, Lady Gaythorne immediately began to exert her voice in a way that perfectly aſtoniſhed Mrs. Conway, who had, till then, heard only the languid tones of affected ſoftneſs proceed from it; nor knew ſhe how to account for the ſudden change, till they approached the orcheſtra, when Lady Gaythorne, fearing they might, any of them, make a pauſe in their walk, ſaid, "No body liſtens to "the muſic this ſeaſon," and quickened her pace. Matilda inſtantly perceived for what reaſon ſhe had talked

ſo

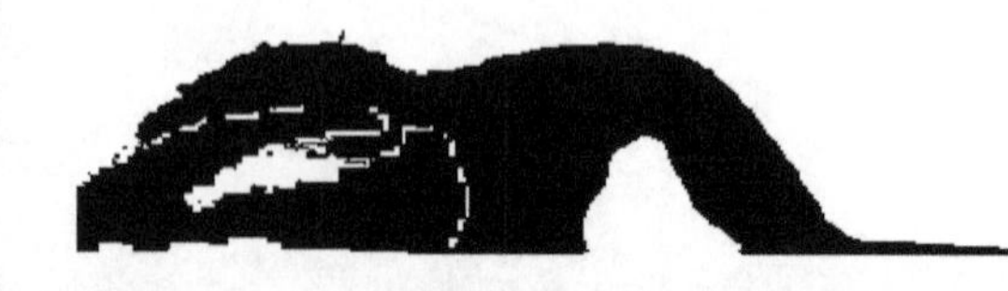

ſo loudly, and ſo faſt, namely, that of convincing every body near enough to be annoyed by her loudneſs, that ſhe was not ſo unfaſhionable as to attend to the muſic.

In a few minutes, a buzzing ſound was heard, which was occaſioned by the entrance of the Prince of ——! And, now, the countenance of every female matron, maiden, prude, or courtezan, was adjuſted to the air conſidered moſt advantageous to the features of each.

The plumage of all expanded; or, (if the expreſſion is deemed objectionable) was ſet in motion: a thouſand graces were thrown into the movements of the heads and necks, and information anxiouſly ſought from every glaſs

pannel,

pannel, concerning the general appearance of the figures that paſſed them. The free unembarraſſed air of Lady Gaythorne, and the ſtyle of her dreſs, which ſolicited obſervation, arreſted the eye of the Prince. For, though the real beauty, and animated intelligence of Mrs. Conway's countenance could not paſs unnoticed, Lady G—— ſooneſt caught, and longeſt rivetted the attention of the votaries of faſhion.

It would be difficult to deſcribe the exultation Lady Gaythorne diſplayed at the general gaze; which the Prince's ſtopping to notice her, had much increaſed, and the triumph of her heart was unbounded, when in a few minutes after, Mr. Needham joined them, exclaiming, " The manners of this age

are

" are without parallel, our young men
" of faſhion have ſo little regard to de-
" cency that they do not ſcruple to
" boaſt their profligate wiſhes reſpect-
" ing women whoſe conduct gives them
" no cauſe for hope. Colonel St.
" Clare has juſt been ſwearing that Sir
" Harry Gaythorne is the moſt uncon-
" ſcionable being in the world, to think
" of monopolizing ſo much elegance
" and beauty. The Prince, he ſays,
" proteſts you are the moſt captivat-
" ing woman he has ſeen to night."

At this information, whether true or falſe, the eyes of Lady Gaythorne ſhot forth the glances of inflated vanity; ſhe even obliged thoſe of whom he had ſpoken, to corroborate what he had ſaid, by looking at them whenever they paſſed her, with that conſcious air that demands particular obſervation. When they were to return home, Lady Gaythorne inſiſted upon Needham's ſupping with them.

During the remainder of the night, though ſhe was in the pleaſanteſt humour imaginable with every one elſe, ſhe was in the worſt humour in the world with Sir Harry.—Indeed, a cloſe obſerver might perceive that ſhe looked upon him as one who had done her an injury by putting a bound to her triumphs, and treated him with the moſt marked indifference.

That perfect perception of politeneſs and delicacy which belonged to Conway, kept him always from running

into

into the too common error of letting, when in company, the object of his particular affections engroſs a diſproportionate ſhare of his attention.—A conduct which generally diſguſts, as it betrays a narrow ſoul, ever bent on gratifying its own propenſities. We enter into ſociety mutually to give and to receive the offices of courteſy; to enliven by the play of wit, to amuſe by the obſervations of ſentiment, or to inſtruct by the documents of experience. But, this cannot be done if our attempts to pleaſe be confined to one object; a mind, elegant and benevolent, revolts from the idea, and would ſooner do violence to its own feelings, than wear the garb of ſelfiſhneſs. Yet, though Conway avoided offending others by particular marks of diſtinction, he never wounded the heart he loved, by neglect.

His respectful attention to Matilda's sentiments, and his looks of approbation, always spoke her to be the object of his highest esteem and affectionate admiration. — A conduct so charmingly delicate and refined, would have insured him the respect of a woman of sense and feeling; but Lady Gaythorne saw it in another light — the rage of conquest glowed with such fury in her breast, that she thought it was not sufficient that no woman should be particularly distinguished in her company; but she deemed it as no more than justice to her charms, that they should all be treated with peculiar marks of neglect whenever she appeared. Of course,

 the

the behaviour of Conway diſpleaſed her; it piqued her pride—and ſhe ſtrove to attract his particular notice, by every alluring wile ſhe had learned in the ſchool of gallantry to enſnare and captivate attention.

After ſupper, when ſhe was requeſted to ſing by Sir Harry, ſhe obſtinately refuſed; Needham and Mrs. Conway united their ſolicitations, yet with no more ſucceſs: but the moment Conway uttered a requeſt, ſhe complied.—This little compliment pleaſed him, perhaps, more than he was conſcious of himſelf, and made him perceive harmony and expreſſion in her warbling he would not have diſcovered without it. She made him chuſe the ſong, and whilſt ſhe ſung it, ſhe appeared to ſee no one but him ; and whether ſhe really excelled herſelf, or that Conway was too much blinded by the charms of the ſinger to be a faſtidious critic, we know not, but he ſeemed really to feel the pleaſure he expreſſed, by a lively ſeizure of her hand, and an enthuſiaſtic repetition of the word, charming !

Matilda was ſurpriſed and ſomewhat hurt ; ſhe had heard his ſentiments the evening before, and ſhe deemed they muſt have been altered by ſome powerful magic, or that Conway had been inſincere enough to affect more pleaſure than politeneſs demanded.

When they were alone, Matilda ſaid to him, " You appeared much delight-

" ed

" ed with Lady Gaythorne's ſong."—
" Yes," replied Conway ; " whether it
" is that ſhe has more ſenſibility than
" we imagined, or that ſhe accidental-
" ly hit upon the true expreſſion of the
" ſong, as an unſkilful ſinger, whilſt
" touching careleſſly the keys of an
" inſtrument, may chance to ſtrike
" ſome note of harmony, I don't pre-
" tend abſolutely to determine ; but, I
" own I could not have believed ſhe
" could have given ſo much pleaſure
" to the mind."

" I ſhould rather ſuppoſe it the effect
" of accident," ſaid Matilda ; " for, I
" cannot believe ſhe can have much
" real ſenſibility, or ſhe could not ſhow
" ſo cruel an indifference to Sir Harry,

" whoſe tenderneſs of heart, and ſweet-
" neſs of manners, ſpeak in his every
" word and action."

" I am inclined to think," returned Conway, " that our friend is not the
" object of her choice; but, rather
" that of an artful mother. If ſo, as
" thoſe inviſible bands are beyond hu-
" man ſkill to form, which draw and
" unite hearts, and our affections are
" not in our own power, is not ſhe more
" to be pitied than blamed, all-accom-
" pliſhed and worthy of her heart, as
" Sir Harry is, that ſhe cannot love
" him."

" Your ſentiment is juſt; but, why,
" my dear Conway, ſhould ſhe not

" ſhow

" ſhow him the eſteem, the reſpect
" that is due to every amiable man
" with whom ſhe is acquainted? female
" delicacy, gratitude, a nice ſenſe of
" honour, juſtice, every tie of duty
" demands this."

" Alas!" ſaid Conway, " we argue
" well upon ſituations in which we are
" not called to act. A long courſe of
" ſuffering of any kind, has, ſome-
" times, the ſalutary effect of impro-
" ving the heart, and giving a philo-
" ſophic turn to the mind, but the
" firſt wounds of the heart generally
" inflame, if they do not feſter it;
" and, when condemned to drag a
" galling chain, it is not to be wonder-
" ed at, if the mind ſometimes loſes

" ſight even of juſtice and of grati-
" tude."

" True," ſaid Matilda, " but I do
" not think ſhe has a ſoul capable
" of true paſſion.—You firſt give her,
" by the aid of imagination, your own
" ſort of mind, and then argue from
" its operations. However, as it is
" not in our power to make our
" friend's lot better by dwelling on
" the ſubject, we will drop it if you
" pleaſe."

" And, whilſt we give a ſigh to his
" fate," ſaid Conway, " let us thank
" Providence who has made our lot ſo
" different."

" Moſt

" Moſt truly, do I," returned Matilda, with energy, every feeling of an affectionate heart revealing itſelf in the ſoftened tone of her voice; " moſt " truly do I."

CHAP. IX.

THEY went the next morning to Mrs. Neville's; Needham met them there: Lady Gaythorne moved with rapidity from room to room; her criticisms were delivered at random, as if she claimed a right without having studied the art she spoke of, to give law to approbation. This is good;—that is bad;— I like this;—I can't bear that;— were her favourite expressions. In the article of drapery, she thought herself qualified to judge beyond any one in the gallery; and, indeed, every one gave her credit for her decision, when she pronounced that the bonnet in which Lady T—— was drawn, was fit only

for

for the head of a chambermaid. However, upon the whole, ſhe liked the pictures ſo well, that ſhe told Mrs. Neville ſhe would ſit with great pleaſure to her pencil.—Mrs. Neville aſked if her ladyſhip had fixed on any hiſtorical ſubject, or if ſhe meant to be drawn ſimply as a portrait.

"Oh! an hiſtorical ſubject by all "means," ſaid her ladyſhip. "We "talked of a great many the other even-"ing; did we not, Mr. Needham?— "what was the laſt?—which was that "I think we concluded would be the "moſt proper."

"Venus introducing Helen to Paris "after his defeat;" ſaid Needham.

"Oh!"

"Oh, yes, ſo it was. Don't you think,
"Mrs. Neville, it will be quite the
"thing?"

"Hah! extremely well choſen;—
"and if your ladyſhip will do me the
"hononr to ſit now, I wilt ſketch in the
"figures."

"But then you will want a Paris,"
exclaimed Needham.

"Perhaps Sir Harry would be kind
"enough to ſit," ſaid Mrs. Neville.

"O! Lard, Mrs. Neville, that will
"be quite ridiculous.—Huſband and
"wife ſitting looking at each other.—
"Heavens! what a ſtupid picture of
"Helen and Paris."

"Come

"Come, Mr. Conway, will you be "the Paris then," ſaid Mr. Needham. "Who that was thought worthy," returned he, "would refuſe to be the "Paris to ſuch a Helen."

This ſpeech, though uttered in the tone of common-place gallantry, hurt Matilda; it recalled to her recollection what had paſſed the night before, and ſhe trembled; for ſhe had a mind, as the reader may have obſerved, that loved to indulge itſelf in philoſophic reflections: and it was an obſervation of hers, that the woman who had power, by whatever means, to remove diſguſt, had a greater chance to enſnare than ſhe who at firſt had attracted a ſlight degree of admiration.

"I don't

"I don't think that Mr. Conway's perſon is in the ſtile of Paris," ſaid Matilda; perhaps hardly knowing what ſhe ſaid.

"Lord," cried Lady Gaythorne, "ſhould it not be an elegant man?"

"Certainly, Madam," returned Mrs. Conway; "but your ladyſhip knows a "man may be handſome, elegant, and "young, and not have the character "of beauty imagination aſſigns to "Paris."

"Very true, Madam," replied Lady Gaythorne; but at the ſame time ſhe looked at Conway with a ſort of a half ſmile, half ſneer, on her face, that ſaid,

"Your

"Your wife will not let you;" and moved away.

We are fory to confefs that the fneer of fuch a being had power to mortify a man of Conway's excellent fenfe; though at the bottom, he certainly could not but be pleafed with the proof this little difplay of Matilda's quick fenfibility gave of the livenefs of her attachment to himfelf. He thought it beft, however, not to feem to enter into the fentiments of either of the ladies; but with that happy prefence of mind which gives perfection to good breeding, he turned to Mrs. Neville, and faid, gaily, "If the Goddefs who is "now to bring Helen and Paris toge-"ther, like that of old, endow but

the

" the youthful warrior with her own
" graces, he cannot fail to pleaſe."

Mrs. Neville bowed, and proceeded to direct the attitudes in which ſhe wiſhed them to place themſelves.

The air Lady Gaythorne aſſumed, though it had not that elegant voluptuouſneſs which ſhould have diſtinguiſhed the fair Grecian, was ſufficiently alluring; for at that moment vanity was mining ten thouſand right feelings in Conway's ſuſceptible heart, and caſt into his countenance an expreſſion not widely diſtant from the ideal character he was to repreſent. Matilda felt a good deal of uneaſineſs, but ſhe ſtrove to examine the pictures, hoping, by that means, her chagrin would be hidden from

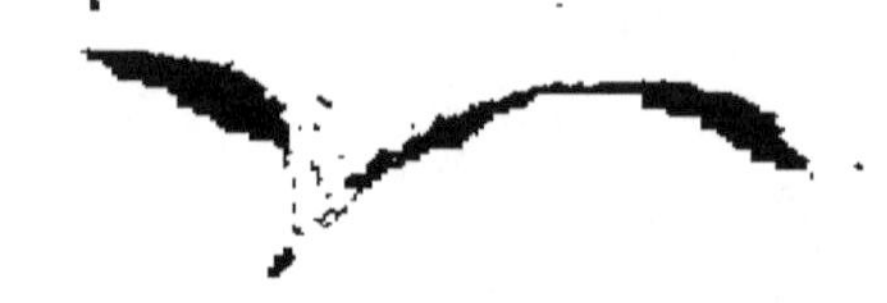

from others; and gladly would ſhe have concealed the cauſe of it even from herſelf. At laſt they departed from Mrs. Neville's, and after taking an airing, returned home to dine.—As ſoon as dinner was over Sir Harry left his friend to go to the Houſe of Commons, an intereſting debate being expected to come on.

Conway went immediately to the drawing-room to ſeek the ladies. He found only Lady Gaythorne there—Mrs. Conway having quitted her to write letters. She was ſitting on a ſopha, with a pair of diamond bracelets in her hand, which, on his entrance, ſhe held to him, and aſked him how he liked them? ſaying, they were juſt ſent from Grey's, and were the preſent of Sir Harry.—

"Beautiful,

" Beautiful indeed !—How happy is
" Sir Harry to have it in his power to
" adorn with ſo much ſplendor the ob-
" ject of his choice," ſaid he, ſeating
himſelf beſide her ; and placing one of
the bracelets on her arm, held her hand
in his to look at it. At that inſtant, with
an expreſſion of *melancholy*, ſhe exclaimed, " What are jewels !"—The air
with which this was ſaid, confirmed Conway in the idea that ſhe had not followed the bent of her own feelings in giving
her hand to Sir Harry ; and the diſtinction with which ſhe had treated him, led
him to think ſhe would have preferred
him. The co-operation of theſe thoughts
produced ſenſations of pity and regard,
that involuntarily led him to preſs the
hand he had in his with a look of ſym-
pathy.—At that moment ſhe threw into
her

her face the look she had practised for Helen, and endeavoured to disengage her hand. He no longer doubted that she had for him a peculiar regard; and he instantly saw in that look a struggle between honour and the heart's affections.

She made a sort of feint to withdraw her hand—he still kept it;—and fired by the rays she darted from her eyes, he drew it eagerly to his lips.—Just then the door opened and Mrs. Conway entered. Her respiration was for a moment suspended; but she quickly recovered herself, and moved to a seat.—Conway was confused and changed colour; but Lady Gaythorne, with perfect composure, said "My dear Mrs. "Conway, I want your opinion of these "bracelets.

" bracelets.—Do you know that Mr.
" Conway has quite affronted me by not
" admiring them;—and ſo he would
" not be convinced that I forgave him
" unleſs I permitted him to ſeal his par-
" don on my hand."

Matilda had by this time ſufficiently recovered herſelf to reply without ſeeming to have beſtowed a ſecond thought on what ſhe had ſeen—" Indeed they " are beautiful, and I ſhould have " thought the taſte and elegance of " the ſetting would have pleaſed him." Matilda's behaviour, contraſted ſo ſtrongly with the ready but pitiful evaſion of Lady Gaythorne, that Conway hated himſelf for having for a moment been dazzled by *her artful* allurements: but the efforts Matilda made to ſuppreſs the appearance of uneaſineſs, made it operate but the more ſtrongly internally.—When ſhe reflected on what had paſſed in the morning, and added to it what ſhe had now ſeen, her heart was agitated with the moſt painful fears.—She ſtrove to join in the converſation, and to appear chearful—but her endeavours to conceal, betrayed the ſtate of her mind more than her ſilence, for ſhe often abruptly dropped the ſubject ſhe had ſtarted, or returned incoherent anſwers to what was addreſſed to her.—Conway, who marked her abſence of mind, was much affected. "Good God!" ſaid he to himſelf, "that a woman whom, "though I cannot but pity on ſome ac-"counts, on others I muſt deſpiſe, ſhould "have had power to cauſe me to give "uneaſineſs

"uneasiness to one of the most amiable
"creatures in the world."

He waited with the anxiety of a lover for an opportunity to relieve the heart of Matilda, and to make his peace with her.

CHAP.

CHAP. X.

AS ſoon as Matilda had retired for the evening, ſhe threw herſelf on a ſopha in her dreſſing-room, and there began to re-contemplate all that had paſſed, and was ſo totally abſorbed in theſe meditations, that Jenny, who ſtood ready with fillets to bind up thoſe locks ſhe had in the morning exhauſted all her art to diſplay, aſked her twice if ſhe ſhould take off her head-dreſs without being heard. Her throat became convulſed, and in a moment tears ſtreamed down her cheeks. Jenny, alarmed, ran inſtantly to the bell, but Matilda ſaid, faintly to her, before ſhe had reached it, "I ſhall be better

“ presently, if you will give me a little
“ water.”

She had a good deal recovered when Conway rapped at the door, and asked if he might be admitted? Matilda wiped her eyes, and cheared her countenance, in the hope he would not perceive she had been weeping. He said he had something to say, and bade Jenny leave the room. He instantly perceived that something had disordered her, and taking hold of her hand with the voice of tenderness, he said, “ You have been
“ ill—tell me what has disordered you.”

“ I had a little hysteric, which soon
“ went off;—I am quite well indeed!”

" No, Matilda," returned he—" no,
" you are not well—ſomething has given
" you uneaſineſs.—If I have been the
" cauſe, ſcruple not to reproach me
" with it.—You know I am not averſe
" to having my faults pointed out to
" me."

" I have ſaid nothing to make you
" think you have been the cauſe of un-
" eaſineſs, and if you had, you know
" I deteſt reproaches—they are too often
" apt to bring on ſevere words that fre-
" quently leave a ſting behind harder to
" endure than the original cauſe of com-
" plaint."

" If you will not tell me, then, in
" what I have been wrong, tell me how

" you would wiſh me to act towards
" you."

" Only to love me every moment of
" your life, as I am ſure I do you."

" Shall I tell you, then, my dear
" girl, how I conſtrue your expreſſions:
" —you think there have been ſome
" moments of my life in which I have
" forgotten you: — perhaps you may
" have drawn this concluſion from ſome
" expreſſion of mine, rather too lively,
" or from ſome little levity of man-
" ner."

Matilda changed colour.

" Confeſs, now, that it was ſo,"
ſaid Conway.

" I will

"I will own," ſaid Matilda, "I have
"already wiſhed we were gotten back
"to our old way of life in the coun-
"try."

"You cannot, Matilda, have more
"pleaſure in the thought of returning,
"than I have; and, you know my mo-
"tive for wiſhing to quit our home;
"was not that of entering into the
"amuſements of a town life."

"Forgive me, Conway, I will no
"longer harbour a thought like diſ-
"truſt:—I ſee you ſtill poſſeſs that
"towering virtue, ſincerity, whoſe am-
"ple ſhade can hide a thouſand faults:
"and did you ceaſe to love me, I am
"ſure you would not ſeek to diſguiſe

 "the

" the change, by acting a continual
" falſehood."

" Ceaſe to love you? Good God!
" can you doubt the exiſtence of a
" flame that has ſo long burnt ſteadily
" though the fluttering of an inſect had
" power to obſtruct the light of it for
" a moment."

" But, we have often ſeen," returned Matilda, " the fluttering of a ſmall
" inſect extinguiſh a clear and lumi-
" nous flame; and the torch of hymen
" once extinguiſhed can never be re-
" newed."

" You continue, Matilda," replied
Conway, " to ſpeak with ſo much ſo-
" lemnity

" lemnity on the subject, that I shall
" think your distrust is fixed."

" Oh, heavens! but, indeed it is
" not," said she: " forgive all that is
" said; I blame my own folly more
" than you can do."

He turned towards her at the supplicating softness of her voice, and holding her to him, " Thus," said he,
" let us mutually seal each others for-
" giveness."

Matilda gave a few tears to their recenciliation, breathing out, " We shall
" soon see our rural home, and our
" lovely children."

"I am ſure," ſaid Conway, "you "cannot have more pleaſure in that "thought than I have; I do not deſire "a town life myſelf, and I ſee that it "does not ſuit with you. You have a "mind too highly wrought to reliſh "the glare of life, and like the ſoft "myrtle, flouriſh beſt in the ſhade."

In a few days the Parliament was adjourned; and the town was emptying apace: Conway now reminded Sir Harry and Lady Gaythorne of their promiſe; and his requeſt that they would immediately put it in execution, being warmly ſeconded by Mrs. Conway, was acceded to.

The ſingularity of Needham's character made Mr. Conway deſire to have

more

more of his company, and as he was a constant visitor at Sir Harry's, and happened to be present when their departure was proposed, he gave him an invitation to go with them; which, though he had an invitation from a peer on his hands, he accepted with avidity, because it was the means of cementing a new acquaiutance, and that was always to him a considerable acquisition.

When they arrived at ———, and were driving through the little park that led to the mansion of Conway, they saw at the root of an old oak their children, with their laps full of the sweetest flowers of the Spring, some of which a female servant who attended them had formed into balls, which they were throwing at one another; whilſt ſhe was fantaſtically adorning them with chaplets artleſsly woven. — Matilda's eyes ſparkled with pleaſure at this ſight. "There are the dear little things," ſhe exclaimed.

Lady Gaythorne remarked the pleaſure with which Conway ſeemed to obſerve this little ebulition of maternal affection. She had perceived that though he had at firſt been ſomewhat dazzled with her light and flippant gaiety—her levity of manner, by being too often repeated till novelty wore away, inſpired him with reflection, and put him upon examining his feelings and guarding againſt their tendencies: this plan not having been ſucceſsful,

Lady

Lady Gaythorne ſet about forming a net of different materials.

But to return.

Soon after they got into the houſe the children were brought in, and all preſent were ſtruck with the notice Lady Gaythorne took of them; the good humoured manner in which ſhe talked to, and endeavoured to amuſe them, made Conway begin to reſume his former opinion that ſhe had naturally a good heart, which had been warped by a wrong education, and too early a commerce with the world.

Even Matilda was pleaſed with her behaviour, though ſhe did not, perhaps, place it to ſo favourable an account, but with a parent's partiality imputed it to the ſuperior beauty and engaging manners of her little ones.

CHAP.

CHAP. XI.

THE next day being Sunday, they went to church. Sir Harry remarked the clergyman as a man of reſpectable appearance, with a clear, unaffected delivery. Mr. Conway replied, that he was a man of a regular, inoffenſive character, of a good underſtanding, and moderately learned. But, that he was much ſtraitened in his circumſtances having a large family, and but very ſlender preferment in the church.

Mr. Williams was the ſon of an innkeeper, who, finding he had a propenſity to letters, bred him to the

church;

church; but died ſoon after he had taken orders, and having ſeveral children, their portions, when the property of the father came to be divided, were very ſmall. Young Williams not having thoſe luminous talents, which in ſpite of all diſadvantages ſometimes recommend an obſcure man to patronage, was forced to exiſt for a few years on a curacy of twenty pounds a year—but marrying a young woman who had ſerved a lady of quality, through her intereſt he obtained a living of about a hundred and fifty pounds a year: upon this, burdened with a family of ſeven or eight children, they now live. Sir Harry ſaid he had it not in his power himſelf to ſerve him, having promiſed the next preſentation of a living in his gift to a gentleman whom he knew at college;

college; but that he would ſpeak to his friend, the Biſhop of ——, in his behalf. — Mr. Conway brought Mr. Williams home to dine with them, and Mrs. Conway ſent to invite Mrs. Williams and the young ladies, to take their tea with them in the afternoon.

This woman was by no means a favourite with Mrs. Conway; but, ſhe choſe to pay her the attentions of a neighbour, out of reſpect to her huſband's character and profeſſion; and often made her preſents, which the narrowneſs of Mr. Williams's income rendered very acceptable to her.

Mrs. Williams was illiterate, conceited, and vain to exceſs; however, ſhe

ſhe had the art of concealing her diſpoſition before thoſe on whom ſhe was dependent. — By ſtudying the humour of the lady ſhe ſerved, entering into her caprices, flattering her beauty, and pretending to admire the moſt faulty parts of her perſon and character, ſhe had lived ſeveral years in great favour in a family where luxury reigned, and œconomy was unknown. She was, of courſe, ill qualified to bring up a family with decency, on an income which required much œconomy in the management of it. Her children ſhowed the ſypmtoms of almoſt total neglect ; when young, they were ſickly, dirty, and fretful ; and when grown up, proud, envious and ignorant. She was ſlatternly at home, and tawdry abroad, for ſhe ſtill retained and indulged her paſſion.

for

for finery;—and, on a Sunday at church, or when paying vifits, fhe ftill exhibited the remains of her lady's caft wardrobe, mixed with fuch inferior additions as her prefent finances allowed her to make.—Too large a portion of the time of Mrs. Williams and her daughters was exhaufted in preparations for vifiting and receiving their acquaintance, to leave much for the neceffary avocations which neatnefs and œconomy demand. Their fociety, which chiefly confifted of a few card-playing old ladies, of fmall fortunes, whofe company was little coveted by either the young, the lively, or the rich; the family of the apothecary they employed, an attorney's wife, or two, and a few ladies whofe hufbands had juft turned their counters into card-tables,

tables, and given their families an opportunity of creeping into the ſociety of the faſhionable circle of a country town.

They ſometimes graced the card and dancing aſſemblies with their preſence; but there was generally ſome ſevere jeſt or other ran through the room, on the ſhabby decorations of the daughters, or the vulgarity of the mother, that ſent them home vexed enough to put them in an ill-humour with every one they found there, without having the ſalutary effect of teaching them the uſeful leſſon of concealing the narrowneſs of their circumſtances, by retiring from public view to purſue leſs expenſive amuſements, and the ſober employments of domeſtic life.

But,

But, though Mrs. Williams frequented the card-tables of ſome few ladies whoſe huſbands had been in trade, with the hope of winning their money, ſhe inſtilled into the minds of her daughters the moſt ſovereign contempt for them; and even many of thoſe whom ſhe now viſited, before their apoſtacy from ſhop-keeping, ſhe had on many occaſions reviled for daring to wear better clothes than herſelf.

I ſaid, when ſhe made her appearance at church ſhe was always equipped in her beſt attire,—but this rarely happened except of an afternoon, for viſiting and card-playing ſwallowed up ſo much of her time in the week days, that ſhe uſually ſpent the Sunday morning

ing in mending in a ſlovenly manner the cloaths of the family.

Mr. Williams would have rejoiced to have ſeen his family better conducted; but he was reſtrained from expreſſing his wiſhes on that head, by the fear of calling forth his wife's eloquence, which, not unfrequently, broke forth in torrents that almoſt overwhelmed him—and upon a ſubject that would have been inexhauſtible had they lived to a patriarchial age, which was her having procured for him the only living he held.

There was one thing, however, in which the good man was reſolute; and that was in taking all his children to church with him, if not prevented by

ſickneſs;

ſickneſs; but this laudable act of authority he could never carry into execution without frequent hints to haſten them. To theſe hints he commonly received ſuch replies as, "Lord, papa, "I can't come yet, for I am drawing "up a hole in Ned's ſtocking: and "I," ſaid another, "am putting a little ink upon Sukey's toe, to hide the "hole in her ſhoe:"—"and I," ſaid a third, "am running up a rent in my "petticoat:"—"and for my part," ſaid a fourth, "I know not that I can "go at all, for Suky has uſed all my "pomatum, and my hair is not half "dreſſed." By this means they were ſeldom ready till too near the hour of appearing in church.—And often when they had ſallied forth, it was a hundred chances to one, but ſome one of them

them difcovered an aperture that necef-fitated the party to run back and get their mother to ftitch up.—This caufed Mr. Williams, at length, to make it a rule, before he paffed over the threfhold, to defire them to examine their clothes; and this circumftance being told rather ludicroufly by one of their fervants, it became a bye word in the parifh? "Come, before we proceed farther let "us examine if there is any thing re-"mains to be fewed."

CHAP.

CHAP. XII.

MRS. Williams came to tea accompanied by her eldeſt daughter; a tall, yellow-complexioned young lady, with a look expreſſive of ſarcaſtic impertinence: her dreſs was an old faſhioned turmeric coloured ſilk gown, flowered with ſhades of red: her petticoat of white luſtring, which had been ſcoured, was trimed with a flounce of waſhed gauze, from below which a dirty green ſtuff peticoat made its appearance: her neck, the texture of which had not been rendered coarſe by too frequent ablutions of water, was decorated by a ſoiled gauze handkerchief, under which her interior drapery was here and there diſcernable,

discernable, and which not being of the whiteſt hue, ſerved like brown powder to heighten the lilies of her complexion.

Soon after they were ſeated, Mrs. Williams aſked who that ſtrange lady was who ſat in farmer Markland's pew.

" Lard, papa, did not you know her?
" Why it is his daughter from London,
" Fanny Markland that was, and drawn
" forth at a prodigious rate I aſſure
" you."

" Why, what had ſhe on, child?" eagerly aſked Mrs. Williams, with great impatience.

" Why, mama, ſhe had on as deli-
" cate a chintz gown as ever you, I ſup-
" poſe,

"pose, would wish to see; and a large
"fashionable bonnet."

"Upon my word," replied the mo-
"ther, "a very fine lady: I declare it's
"a shame: but farmers' daughters now
"dress as fine as gentlewomen; nay,
"one can't distinguish them from real
"ladies."

"Not perhaps, in public places,"
returned Mrs. Conway; "but a real
"gentlewoman can be imitated by vul-
"gar people only in dress; her conver-
"sation and deportment will always
"shew, that a liberal education, mani-
"fested in her superior complacence and
"elegance of manners, forms such an
"essential difference, as no dress, how-
"ever œconomical, can hide; and for

" the want of which no drefs, however
" rich and ftudied, can compenfate."

" You are perfectly right, Madam,"
faid Mifs Anne ; " I dare fay fhe is a
" vulgar creature when you come to
" talk with her."

" Indeed, Anne, fhe did not look *fo*,"
faid Mrs. Williams.

" What perfon is it you fpeak of,
" Mifs Williams? " faid Mrs. Conway.

" Why, Madam," replied fhe, " it is
" the daughter of a farmer whom Lady
" Witlington took a fancy to, from be-
" ing fhewn fome of her drawings when
" fhe was a fchool girl, and her ladyfhip
" took her to live with her ; but to be
" fure,

" ſure, you know ſhe could be nothing
" but a ſervant, Sir," turning to Need-
" ham, who ſat next to her.

" No, Madam," replied he, very ſen-
tentiouſly, " indeed, I do not know."

Miſs Anne was a little diſconcerted,
but ſoon reſumed her converſation—
" And ſo, Madam, as I have been told,
" ſhe is married, and gets her living by
" painting."

" Perhaps," ſaid Mrs. Williams, with
the quick reſpiration of envious alarm,
" perhaps, though ſhe may get a great
" deal of money; for I remember when
" I lived as companion to Lady D———,
" her ladyſhip had her picture drawn,
" and it coſt a vaſt deal of money, and

" all the great people took notice of the
" painter."

" Oh, Yes," cried Miſs Williams;
" but that muſt have been a capital
" hand, not ſuch an inſignificant crea-
" ture as Mrs. Neville."

" Very true, child," ſaid Mrs. Williams, her anxiety a little compoſed; " I
" dare ſay, nobody takes any notice of
" her."

" Oh! no, mama, I dare ſay not:
" you know one hears the names of all
" the great painters mentioned in the
" public prints; but one never hears of
" Mrs. Neville, as a perſon of great
" abilities, you know, Sir."

" Yes,

"Yes, Madam," replied Needham, "the name of Mrs. Neville is often "mentioned with respect; though her "fame, which began among the higher "class of people, has not yet descended "to the vulgar.

"Mrs. Neville is the lady who is to "paint your ladyship's picture, is she "not," said Mrs. Conway, turning to Lady Gaythorne.

"Yes," said Lady Gaythorne, "I be-"lieve she is; but I don't perfectly re-"collect—Is she the same person, Mr. "Needham?"

"There is but one lady who paints "of that name," he replied.

"Upon my word," said Mrs. Conway, "when I saw her at Lady Gay-"thorne's, and afterwards at her own "house, I thought her a very pleasing "woman, and one who had conversed "with, and acquired the manners of "the best company."

The Williams seemed thunder struck, and their wonder was heightened when Lady Gaythorne, who had a wish to convince even the family of a little country clergyman, that she never condescended to notice persons whom "no-"body knows," now exerted herself sufficiently to say, "The first time La-"day Witlington introduced her to me, "was at Lady Bell Gray's assembly."

The

The Williams could now ſcarcely breathe, ſo much were they aſtoniſhed.

"Well, indeed, 'tis amazing," ſaid Miſs Williams; "why, do you know "her father is only a very middling "farmer—but ſome people have ſuch "luck—"

"Luck, indeed," cried Mrs. Williams: "why now, my daughter, I do "aſſure you, you went to the very ſelf-"ſame boarding-ſchool as ſhe did, and "was there, indeed, as much as a year, "or more, longer than this girl; and "learnt drawing of the ſelf-ſame iden-"tical maſter, and was exceedingly "apt and clever too; and you ſee why "ſhe had not luck to meet with any one "to notice her. Well, people may

"very well ſay it is better to be born
"fortunate than rich."

"I wonder none of our family ob-
"ſerved her at church;—I wiſh I had
"ſeen her," ſaid Mrs. Conway.

"In your pew, Madam," ſaid Mrs. Williams, "you could not ſee her; and
"in going from church, I remarked
"that ſhe walked immediately home
"with her father, without ſtaying to
"ſpeak to any body."

"I proteſt," exclaimed Needham, who ſat on a ſtool in the window, "I
"do believe that the lady who is now paſſing the gate is Mrs. Neville!"

"It

"It is, I really think," said Mrs. "Conway;—"I wish she would call "here. If we were to walk round, and "go out at the little door in the park "walk, we should meet her, and we "might then invite her in.

"The shower that has fallen has "made the grass wet—and I think it "would be very improper for you to "walk," said Conway.

"Do you think so?" said Mrs. Conway.

"Oh dear—I wish we could go," said Lady Gaythorne, with an earnestness which, whether real or affected, pleased Conway.

 "Upon

"Upon my word, I would not have "you venture, ladies," ſaid Conway ;— "but if Mr. Needham pleaſes, we will "go ; and as he is an old acquaintance, "perhaps we may both together prevail "upon her to overlook the etiquette of "your going to pay her the firſt viſit, "and to favour us with her company "for an hour or two."

"Go then, directly," ſaid Mrs. Conway, and immediately they ſnatched up their hats, and ſet out. They preſently returned with Mrs. Neville. The moment they came into the houſe, Mrs. Conway roſe from her ſeat, and, quick as thought, opened the door of the room in which they were ſitting, and held it till Conway introduced Mrs. Neville; when taking her hand with a low curtſey,

curtsey, she said, "This is extremely "kind," and led her to the top of the room. The respect with which Mrs. Conway treated her visitor, and the polite ease with which she received these marks of attention, convinced the Williams that they were not new to her, and inspired the most pungent heart-burning.. The conversation turned on the fine arts and polite literature. Conway shewed Mrs. Neville, and asked her opinion of a little collection of pictures he had made from some of the best masters, ancient and modern. But this conversation was soon interrupted; and by the address of Lady Gaythorne, the diversions of the town became the topic, in which Mrs. Neville bore no inconsiderable part, to the great mortification of Mrs. Williams and her daughter, who were conſtrained by dire neceſſity to be totally ſilent:—ſo that, unable to bear the ſcene any longer, Mrs. Williams ſoon took her leave, impatient to have an opportunity of unburthening her mind to her daughter. Mrs. Neville ſtaid after them, and partook of a little ſupper;—the converſation held, at it was ſeaſoned by the ſalt of attic wit, and elegant pleaſantry.

With all that Mrs. Neville ſaid, Lady Gaythorne had the addreſs to ſeem pleaſed, and treated her with ſo much attention and reſpect, that Conway was charmed with the proof, as he thought, this gave of a mind naturally liberal; and he could not help exclaiming when they were alone, to Mrs. Conway, "How invaluable a bleſſing is a juſt

"education,

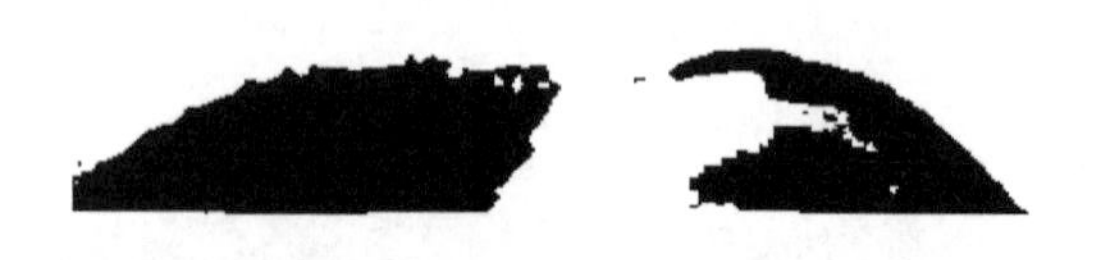

" education, and how liable are the beſt-
" diſpoſed minds to be warped by a bad
" one!"

CHAP.

CHAP. XIII.

THE next morning, when they walked out, Conway walked with Lady Gaythorne; and Needham and Sir Harry ſtrolled on before with Mrs. Conway.— "Is Mrs. Conway ill?" ſaid Lady Gaythorne; "ſhe looks quite indiſpoſed to-"day."

"She is uneaſy about one of her chil-"dren."

"Is ſhe?" replied Lady Gaythorne: "—I wonder ſhe did not mention it at "breakfaſt!"

"Oh

" Oh no," faid he, " Matilda is of
" all human beings the leaft inclined to
" let others partake of her troubles;—
" though at all times ready to commu-
" nicate her comforts and her joys."

" You give her a charming charac-
" ter :"—" Indeed fhe is deferving of
" it," he returned.

" Oh, I have no doubt of it," cried
fhe; " for Sir Harry told me you mar-
" ried for love;—and in that cafe, I
" fuppofe, if fhe had but few merits,
" your imagination would fupply them;
" —at leaft, if the fame partiality con-
" tinues after marriage,—which I fhould
" like to know from one who had really
" felt what is called a romantic paffion."

This

This frank, though indirect avowal, of her not having married under the influence of an affectionate attachment, struck Conway for some moments silent. He felt for the fate of his friend —he felt there was an indelicacy in her confession; but in another moment he found himself inclined to excuse, rather than blame her; and to look upon it as the unguarded ebulition of a too incautious heart, by reflecting on the manners of the country in which she had resided, and the sentiments in which she had been educated. He remained absorbed in thought, till she reiterated with an appearance of frankness and simplicity that interested him.

"I should like to have the question

answered

anſwered by one who had really experi-
" enced a true paſſion."

" A true paſſion, madam," replied Conway, who began to recover a more diſengaged manner," " never departs
" from the heart, though after unin-
" terrupted poſſeſſion of the object, it
" takes a new, but not leſs pleaſing,
" form.—Nor is it difficult to account
" for the change. Before marriage, the
" lover, even if he be an acknowledged
" one, has, comparatively, few oppor-
" tunities of enjoying the ſociety of his
" miſtreſs. In thoſe ſhort moments he
" has a thouſand fears to relate on his
" own part—a thouſand doubts to clear
" up on her's; and ſcarcely has he felt
" the tear of reconiliation, or the preſ-
" ſure of endearment, before the mo-
" ment

" ment of ſeparation arrives, and he
" goes away at laſt, reproaching his too
" treacherous memory with having for-
" gotten a thouſand things he had to ſay.
" Thus grief, joy, hope, deſpair, per-
" plexity and delight, alternately ſway
" his breaſt, and keep it in continual tu-
" mult. Poſſeſſion calms this perturba-
" tion, and inſpires an affection that fills
" without agitating the ſoul;—its rap-
" tures are leſs tumultuous, becauſe its
" anxieties are fewer:—yet, let but an
" incident occur to place in a new or
" ſtronger light ſome virtue, grace or
" accompliſhment of the object of his
" affections; let ſickneſs or calamity me-
" nace the loſs of her, and wedded love
" inſtantly proves its energy by kindling
" to tranſport, or ſinking to deſpair."

" On

" On my word," ſaid Lady Gay-
" thorne, " you made an exquiſite de-
" ſcription.—How much muſt they loſe
" who never knew the charms of ſuch
" a ſtate !"

There was a ſomething in her manner of ſaying this which, as it had the appearance of real ſenſibility, melted the heart of Conway. " To change the
" ſubject," cried he, " Do you ſee
" that farm houſe which ſtands ſo pleaſ-
" ingly on that hill before us ?—It is the houſe where Mrs. Neville's father lives."

" Let us go and return her viſit," ſaid ſhe. Conway was pleaſed with her propoſal, and ſtepping to Mrs. Conway, he ſaid " Lady Gaythorne wiſhes us to
" lengthen

"lengthen our walk, and call upon
"Mrs. Neville.

"But I am fearful," said Lady Gaythorne, "that it will fatigue Mrs. Conway, as she seems not well."

"Oh, not at all:—I shall be very
"happy to return her visit."

When they arrived at the gate of the fold yard of the farm, they were met by a venerable looking man of about sixty, with the implements of husbandry upon his shoulder, and whose athletic frame and healthful countenance spoke the temperance and activity of his life.—They inquired if Mr. Neville was at home. Parental joy animated his open aspect, and with a bend of his body that

that had in it the graceful ſimplicity of patriarchal times, he thanked them for the honour they did him, and offered to conduct them to the houſe. In their approach to the houſe, Mrs. Markland came forth to meet them.—She was a fair and comely woman, of an age ſuitable to that of the farmer; and, like her huſband, had that primitive plainneſs of deportment, which, even to thoſe who have ſeen the manners of courts, conveys an idea of dignity, becauſe compoſed, recollected, and unembarraſſed: —their civilities were not a barbarous mixture of ruſtic ignorance and an affectation of the factitious mode of behaviour of people in higher life, but the ſimple manners of their anceſtors, in which they had been bred, and which cuſtom had rendered natural to them.

Mrs.

Mrs. Markland bid a ſervant tell Mrs. Neville that Mr. and Mrs. Conway were come to ſee her, and conducted her gueſts into a large old-faſhioned parlour, whoſe floor and furniture had the poliſh of domeſtic neatneſs.

They ſaid ſomething to the good reſpectable matron in praiſe of her daughter.

"You honour her much," ſhe returned.—"She has been a great deal in the "world; and it is long, very long, "ſince I ſaw her, till ſhe came down "this ſummer to us.—We find her ſtill "humble, and kind, and dutiful, as "when ſhe firſt left us; but ſhe is not "the ſame in other reſpects;—her "health, her ſpirits are gone! My

"girl,

" girl, when ſhe left us, was like the
" gayeſt bird that flies:—I am afraid,
" but I dare not aſk her queſtions, for
" ſhe always ſhifts the ſubject.—I am
" afraid ſhe has not the beſt huſband;—
" but ſhe never complains; ſhe has not
" a heart that will bear much unkind-
" neſs,—her conſtitution is already bro-
" ken; and I fear her heart will ſoon
" follow. Lady Witlington, to be ſure,
" has frequently written to us to tell us
" how happily our daughter was ſettled,
" and to expreſs her pleaſure at it:—
" but alas! our child ſays nothing, but
" that ſhe is content. Perhaps you may
" know him, madam," ſaid ſhe to Mrs.
Conway, " and can tell us how he be-
" haves, for we have never ſeen him;—
" we may, perhaps, do him an injuſtice
" —but we have heard that men in the
" gay

"gay world act in a manner, and think
"nothing of it, that would break my
"poor girl's heart. Why did we ever
"part with her!—but we thought it
"was for the beſt.—I know ſhe is not
"happy, for the other day ſhe plucked
"a large bunch of cypreſs, and placed
"two or three of the ſmalleſt roſe buds
"ſhe could find in the midſt of it;—ſhe
"ſighed, and ſaid it was emblematic of
"her life. I did not underſtand her at
"the time, but afterwards, when we
"were looking at her paintings, ſhe
"told us that cypreſs ſignified *mourning*,
"and roſes *pleaſure*; and *ſmall* were the
"buds that ſhe placed among the cy-
"preſs ſhe wore in her boſom."

The company avoided giving the good woman pain, by ſaying they had not

not long had the pleaſure of knowing Mrs. Neville, and were not intimate enough to have ſeen any thing of her domeſtic ſituation. The converſation was interrupted by the appearance of Mrs. Neville, who entered with that quiet eaſe which diſtinguiſhed her deportment. She expreſſed her pleaſure at ſeeing them, and then they entered into an agreeable converſation.

Lady Gaythorne ſeemed delighted with the ſituation of the houſe, and drawing a chair oppoſite to a window that commanded a beautiful proſpect of a romantic country, with the Avon ſtealing along at the bottom of the hill on which the houſe ſtood; "I could live "here for ever," ſaid ſhe, affecting a tone of enthuſiaſm.

Needham ſmiled, and leaning over the back of her chair, "I remember," ſaid he, "Sterne ſomewhere ſays, that the "expreſſion *the world*, frequently means "only the little circle in which a man "moves, and is as often uſed (when he "ſpeaks of the obſervations made on his "actions) by him who never goes be- "yond the ſmoke of his own little vil- "lage, as by him whoſe deeds or whoſe "talents have extended his fame to di- "ſtant climes. In my opinion the ex- "preſſion *for ever* is often as ridicu- "louſly applied. The coxcomb, who "having received an encouraging billet "from his miſtreſs, proteſts he will pre- "ſerve it *for ever*;—means, till it is "worn out by being conſtantly carried "in his pocket, and boaſtfully ſhewn to "every one he meets. When a notable

"lady

" lady ſays ſhe has bought a gown that
" will laſt *for ever*, ſhe only means the
" term of a few months: and when a
" town lady declares ſhe could look at
" a proſpect for ever, ſhe means, I
" ſhould preſume, for *ten minutes*.

" We ſhall be able to judge of your
" ladyſhip's idea of *for ever*, when we
" have the pleaſure of paying Mrs. Ne-
" ville an afternoon viſit," cried Mrs.
" Conway." Mrs. Neville bowed and
ſaid, ſhe hoped they would do her that
honour very ſoon."

" Oh, I ſhould like better than any
" thing in the world, to come here this
" evening," returned Lady Gaythorne:
" —are you otherwiſe engaged, Mrs.
" Neville?

Mrs. Neville aſſured her ladyſhip ſhe was diſengaged, and ſhould rejoice in the honour of ſeeing them. It was then agreed that they ſhould take their tea at Mr. Markland's.

"We can then," ſaid Mr. Conway, "ſhew to Sir Harry and Lady Gay-"thorne a ſpot at the diſtance of two or "three fields from this houſe, worthy "of obſervation, as being the birth-"place of the inimitable Butler, author "of Hudibras. Stratford has been "eternized for giving birth to Shake-"ſpeare; and, had I a pen that could "give immortality, the little village of "Strenſham ſhould live for ever.

"Is there any thing curious in the "houſe itſelf?" aſked Lady Gaythorne.

"Nothing

" Nothing at all," replied Mrs. Neville, " it is a low-roofed, thatched cot-
" tage, which was the property of But-
" ler's father :—a piece of ground that
" belongs to it is ſtill called Butler's
" Cloſe. I viſited the little dwelling this
" morning, for the first time ſince my
" childhood), with a high degree of en-
" thuſiaſtic pleaſure. A poor cottager
" lives in one part of it ; the other is
" uninhabited, and quite out of repair.
" The largeſt room is a tolerable ſized
" kitchen. *Here*, (thought I, as I ſtood
" beſide the fire place, looking at ſome
" old brick-work, which ſufficiently
" ſpoke the antiquity of the building)
" *Here* ſat, after the labours of a toil-
" ſome day, the reſpectable yeoman ;—
" *there* the contented companion of his
" induſtry. Imagination inſtantly paint-

 " ed

" ed a groupe of happy faces in each
" of the wide-extended, ſocial chimney
" corners: the principal figure ſtands
" forward with a boldneſs of relief that
" rivets attention; not diſtinguiſhed by
" outward garb, or high-bred graces:
" but by the flexible features of genuine
" humour, and the ſparkling glances of
" pointed wit. The moral tale goes
" round; the 'crackling faggot blazes
" on the chearful hearth.' I liſten to
" the arch commentaries of the youthful
" ſatiriſt on the little tranſactions of the
" village; the comic alluſions that fall
" from him in language, quaint, yet
" pictureſque! I ſee the ludicrous, the
" vivid images his ſportive fancy raiſes!
" and I feel the little dome ſhake with
" the unreſtrained burſt of ruſtic laugh-
" ter! A penſive traveller, who has
" forſaken

" forſaken the ſpot where he gave to the
" tomb the remains of a beloved part-
" ner, and is rambling to diſſipate a
" gloom bordering upon deſpair, ap-
" proaches.—He feels, for the firſt time
" ſince that ſad event, his heart accord
" to the tones of hilarity; and by an
" involuntary motion checks the reins
" of his horſe: he is dubious of the
" road he ought to take, in order to
" reach a place of abode for the night.
" He diſmounts to make inquiries,—
" and whilſt he faſtens his horſe to the
" little wicket in the hedge which
" fences the cottage from the high road
" experiences a pleaſure long unknown
" to his breaſt, in the thought of look-
" ing in upon a groupe of joyous coun-
" tenances. I don't know how far I
" ſhould have purſued the idea, had not

 " a little

" a little girl I had with me, who, poor
" child, ſaw nothing but a fireleſs
" hearth, an unpaved floor, and bare
" walls, by aſking me how much longer
" I meant to continue in that dirty
" place, awaked me from my reverie."

" Oh, I ſhall like to go extremely;
" but I am afraid I ſhall ſee no ſuch vi-
" ſions," cried Lady Gaythorne. They
ſoon after took their leave and departed.

In returning they were overtaken by
a ſhower of rain, as they were croſſing
a wide field; and in order to ſhelter
themſelves, ran into a little ſhed, built
for the herdſmen to retreat to in bad
weather. Here they had not long been
before Mrs. Williams and her two
daughters came up: the genlemen inſtantly

ſtantly ſurrendered their places to them, and endured the beating of the ſtorm under a hedge.

CHAP. XIV.

WHILST the Williams ſtood here, they heard, to their infinite mortification, that the family from Conway park had been viſiting Mrs. Neville. As ſoon as the ſtorm was over they took leave, and purſued their different walks: but the pride of Miſs Williams had received a deep wound, and ſhe ſaid to her mother as they returned home; "I am aſto-
" niſhed the creature could have the ef-
" frontery to invite ſuch a perſon as
" Lady Gaythorne to drink tea at a
" farm houſe—but ſome people's aſ-
" ſurance carries all before it; for
" people that are polite, can't tell how
" to refuſe their bold requeſts.—Mama,

"I think after this, you cannot ſcruple "to invite them to your houſe."

"Why, truly Anne," ſaid ſhe, "if "farmer Markland can take the liberty "of aſking Sir Harry and Lady Gay-"thorne, to drink tea with them, I "think we may: and I am ſure Mrs. "Conway would far prefer viſiting us."

"Yes, indeed, mama, I think we may; "but now we know they have viſited "her, it will look as if we imitated her, "to aſk them to drink tea: I ſhould "like for them to dine with us: "that would ſhew we are of more con-"ſequence.—To be able to give a din-"ner to Sir Harry and Lady Gaythorne, "would give us quite an eclat."

"Lord! child," replied the mother, "but great people have every thing in "ſuch a ſtile, that we ſhall look quite "ſhabby and mean."

"Oh, never fear, mama: Colonel "Morgan's houſekeeper will lend us any "thing we may want to ſet off the ta- "ble; and we can have John Maſon's "ſon to wait; and that little green coat "of Jack's (which is laid by becauſe "he has out grown it) will do for Nick "Maſon to wear for the day very well; "and I can find a bit of red cloth ſome- "where in the houſe to tack on for a "collar and cuffs; and with the red "waiſtcoat he has got of his own, we "can make him look very ſpruce."

"Lord

"Lord! child, but he is ſuch a queer-looking lank-haired numps."

The motion of Miſs Anne was received with approbation; and it was agreed nem. con. to ſend an invation that very evening. A meſſenger was immediately diſpatched to the next town to purchaſe ſome dinner cards: in the interval, Miſs Anne buſied herſelf in facing the little green coat: and having no red thread in the houſe, ſhe made uſe of ſome blue, which, if it did not add to the neatneſs of the garment, certainly contributed to make that variety, which is allowed to be the ſoul of ornament. By the time the boy returned, the coat was ready for him to put on, in which he was ordered immediately to equip himſelf, and not to forget

get to ſhake the flour-box over his head. Mean while Miſs Anne adorned his hat with a yellow button, and a bit of tarniſhed gold lace; which having performed, ſhe ſat down, and after ſpoiling ſeveral cards, at laſt compleated one, and ſent Nicholas with it, ordering him to return with all poſſible expedition, as no time was to be loſt in making the neceſſary preparations.

The door of Mr. Conway's houſe was opened by Sir Harry's French valet, who much diverted with the figure of the boy, could hardly take the card from him without laughing; but, checking his riſibility whilſt he ſurveyed the marks of ſome fullers earth, which had been rubbed upon the coat, in order to diſ-

charge

charge the greafe, and which had not fufficiently dried to be brufhed off clean.

"Ah! monfieur, faid he, you have "had un little tomber in de dirt— "come you wid me."

So faying he carried him to the reft of the fervants, who no fooner faw poor little Nick Mafon fo metamorphofed, than they burft into an univerfal laugh: not being able to ftand this, the boy took to his heels and ran off.

The moment the family at the parfonage fet their eyes upon him, they cried as with one voice, "Where is the "card?"

"I have

"I have brought no card," replied Nick; "they were not at home, so I "know not whether they will come or "not; but however, this I know, if "they laugh as mainly at poor folks "when they be dreſſed up a bit as their "ſervants do, their room is better than "their company."

The Williams were aſtoniſhed, and ſomewhat diſconcerted at the expreſſions of the boy; in which ſtate we requeſt to leave them for the preſent, and return to the Conways and their viſitors.

CHAP.

CHAP XV.

" I DON'T know when I have made " a more agreeable viſit," ſaid Mrs. Conway, as the little party ſeated themſelves after returning from Mr. Markland's, " the pleaſing converſation of " Mrs. Neville, the intereſtingneſs of " her appearance in a ſtraw hat and " linen gown, the unaffected ſimplicity " with which we were entertained by " the good old people, the cleanly " looks of the roſy ſervant who waited " at tea and ſerved us with the delicate " fruits and cream, the order and " cleanlineſs of every thing in the " houſe, and the quietneſs and regula- " rity with which every one ſeemed

" to

" to be following their avocations as
" we walked through the fimple dwel-
" ling, gave a picture of refpectable
" induftry that infpired the moft pleafing
" fenfations,"

" Oh, I was charmed," drawled out lady Gaythorne in an affected tone,
" there was fomething in the whole
" extremely nouvelle."

" And, did you really enjoy it, Char-
" lotte," faid Sir Harry.

" Oh, intirely," faid fhe.

" What cards are thefe," faid Mrs. Conway chancing to caft her eyes on the chimneypiece : — " From Mrs.
" Williams :—Will it be agreeable to
" your

" your ladyſhip to accept the invita-
" tion?"

" Oh, by all means," ſaid ſhe. And Mrs. Conway immediately diſpatched an anſwer, which communicated no ſmall delight to the Williams's family,—who had been on the rack of anxiety to know how their invitation would be received.

When the hour of viſiting arrived, in ſpite of the previous commands and menaces of their mother, the five younger children of the Williams could not help popping their heads out of the upper windows, like pigeons peeping from their holes.

The

The dreſs of Lady Gaythorne, which roſe to the extreme point of the faſhion, ſtruck a kind of awe into the two elder daughters, who, with their mother, were ready to receive them. Little converſation paſſed before dinner, for Miſs Anne and her ſiſter were ſo overpowered by the glitter of Lady Gaythorne's appearance that ſhe could not become collected enough, for ſome time, to ſtart any ſubject, or to join in any one that was begun; and Mrs. Williams, on her part, was inceſſantly making excurſions to the kitchen to give directions concerning, and to inſpect the cookery that was going forward. Her huſband endeavoured to ſupply her place, but he gave them pain by the anxiety which they plainly perceived in his countenance leſt his family

family ſhould render themſelves ridiculous by ill-conducting the entertainment. The boy, at laſt, appeared with the firſt diſh, the wildneſs of his eyes, his trepidation, his ſhabby livery, and aukward gait, were ſo truly ludicrous, that their viſirors could hardly refrain from laughing. The dinner conſiſted of unneceſſary variety of proviſions, very ill dreſſed, and from the want of attendants, and the ſcarcity of utenſils, very ill-ſerved up. The poor lad, in his hurry to give Lady Gaythorne a glaſs of wine, ſpilled it on her apron; but as ſhe did not ſeem to feel any concern at the accident, Mrs. Williams bore it with chriſtian meekneſs, giving him but a ſhort reprimand; which, conſidering ſhe excelled more in the flowery and diffuſe ſtile of eloquence, than in the laconic,

was

was rather furprifing;—but, upon his letting half a dozen beautiful china plates fall out of his hands, fhe was miftrefs of no fuch forbearance, for this accident touched her nearly; they were all of them borrowed, and fhe muft of neceffity replace them at a confiderable expence. Mr. Williams, and Mifs Anne in vain begged her to be calm: her choler was roufed, and fhe could not refrain from venting it upon the poor trembling boy; who heartily wifhed himfelf out of his green jacket and quietly following the plough. When the torrent would have ceafed we know not, had not a fudden outcry like that of children whom fome accident had befallen (and which feemed to proceed from an out-houfe) alarmed them. Sir Harry, who fat next the window,

window, which was but a ſhort ſtep from the ground, popped out and opened the door of the place from whence the ſound had iſſued; and diſplayed to the company, who had by this time gone forth much terrified, the cauſe of the terrible howling they had heard, which was, two or three of Mrs. Williams's children, who had been locked up there, one of whom in trying to get out, had bruiſed his fingers with the door; this afforded a new ſubject for the eloquence of Mrs. Williams, who called inſtantly for the cook (as ſhe ſtiled the woman whom they had called in to aſſiſt them in dreſſing the victuals) and the other maid. Only the cook appeared, however, of whom ſhe demanded who had locked up the children in that ſtrange place; and why they

they had not been left in the nurſery with the reſt?

" Lord bleſs your heart, Madam," returned the woman, who, fired at the haughty manner in which Mrs. Williams interrogated, " why, what could " I do? Deuce a bit would they ſtay " in the chamber along with the big " ones, for they makes it a rule always " to plague the little ones; and there " they were under my feet or in the " dripping pan every minute.—So I " took and put them in there out of " the way."

" But, Dolly ought to have minded " them, mama," ſaid Miſs Williams, " for what could ſhe have to do,—

" when

"when we have a footboy to wait at
"table."

"Lord keep you, Miſs," replied the woman, "the poor girl has had enough
"to do, what with running here and
"there, and having the children bawl-
"ing and ſqualling about her ears;
"and it's as much as ever ſhe can do
"to keep 'em out of the parlour."

Miſs Anne, who ſtood upon thorns, and was in the moſt terrible ſtate of mortification, deſired the woman to take all the children into the nurſery, and tell Dolly to take care of them.

"Why, Miſs," ſaid the woman, who was much irritated at the commanding and inconſiderate language of

Miſs Anne, "I'll tell her ſo to do,
"when ſhe comes back; but ſhe is
"gone to try to borrow ſome plates,
"in lieu of thoſe Nick broke."

The company could not help pitying the aukward ſituation of the William's, who uttered a thouſand apologies to their gueſts for their having been ſo diſagreeably diſturbed, and delivered many invectives againſt ſervants, as they returned to the parlour.

But ſcarcely had they reſeated themſelves at table, and Mrs. Williams put her knife into a currant tart, before a violent rumbling over head like the noiſe of thunder, alarmed them all.—Lady Gaythorne ſtartled, fell back in her ſeat, and ſeemed to faint. Whilſt

4 ſome

ſome were employed in recovering the fainting lady, others ran up ſtairs to the chamber from whence the noiſe came, which was uſed as a lumber room, and for the children to play in during wet weather, or when Mrs. Williams received company. Here they beheld five or ſix children wheeling an old broken little coach about the room.

The gentlemen turned the matter off with a laugh at the oddity of the accident; and Mrs. Conway, with the kindeſt tone of voice in the world, ſaid ſhe was delighted "the little creatures had "not hurt themſelves."

But not ſo ſpoke Lady Gaythorne, whoſe nerves were ſo totally deranged by the ſucceſſive hurries they had undergone, that as ſoon as the cloth was removed, ſhe begged them to excuſe her leaving them, ſaying ſhe was ſo ill as to be unable to ſtay longer, and requeſted Sir Harry to order the carriage. Mrs. Conway inſiſted, as ſhe was ſo ill, to accompany her home.

CHAP.

CHAP. XVI.

WHEN they came home Lady G— retired to her own apartment to compoſe herſelf; and Matilda amuſed herſelf with the children till the gentlemen returned. When they entered, Mrs. Conway told Sir Harry, that Lady Gaythorne was gone to endeavour to get a little ſleep, and that ſhe believed ſhe was not ſtirring. He ſoon after went out of the room, as did Needham; when Matilda ſaid to Mr. Conway, "I was quite "diſtreſſed to be obliged to leave the "Williams immediately after that ri-"diculous accident; for it muſt hurt "poor Mrs. Williams extremely, to "think the troubleſomeneſs of her chil-

" dren drove her visitors away: but it
" was impossible for me to avoid insist-
" ing upon attending the sick lady
" home;—for my part, I confess I
" thought the scene had infinitely more
" of the comic than the tragic in it."

"People view things," returned Conway, "in different lights, according to
" the various casts of their minds. I
" declare, I really think it might take
" the effect it apparently had on Lady
" Gaythorne, upon almost any woman
" who had no taste for humour, and
" was unused to see occurrencies of the
" kind."

"Well," replied Matilda, "truth
" obliges me to confess, I think her
" terrors were wholly assumed; but,
" admitting

" admitting them to be real, ought ſhe
" not in politeneſs, in good nature, to
" have endeavoured to have concealed
" them from the parties concerned, who
" ſhe muſt perceive were in a very pi-
" tiable ſituation?"

" Indeed, Matilda, I think you judge
" the actions of Lady Gaythorne too
" ſeverely."

" Good Heavens! Mr. Conway, I
" could never have thought to have
" heard you the defender of affectation."

" Nor do you at preſent, Matilda,"
replied Conway; " but ſuppoſing her
" ladyſhip's illneſs to be really aſſumed,
" you are certainly too partial in your
" ſtrictures. Do not the fooliſh attempts

" of the Williams equally entitle them
" to the reproach of ridiculous affecta-
" tion, of what is entirely out of their
" power to appear ?"

" Yes ; but my pity for their narrow
" circumftances made me refrain from
" commenting on their folly."

" But then, fhould not your pity for
" the wrong education of this young
" woman have induced you to have
" thrown the fame kind veil over her
" defects.

" There was a time," faid Matilda,
" when you were of my opinion, and
" when you thought that——"

" Yes,"

"Yes," interrupted he, "but that "was before I had reflected on the dif-"advantages ſhe had laboured under; "before I had ſeen ſeveral little turns in "her mind, which, ſhining through "the ravages of diſſipation, have prov-"ed to me that ſhe has naturally an "amiable heart."

"I have done, Conway," ſaid Matilda, "nor will I ever attempt to argue the "matter further; for I ſee you do not "wiſh to be convinced of what appears "to me perfectly clear."

"I am aſtoniſhed, Matilda," ſaid Mr. Conway; "I never before ſaw you ſo "ſlow to be convinced of an error; nor "ſo quick to ſee the faults of another."

" Nor do I ever recollect the time," replied ſhe, " when our opinions of " any perſon were ſo different, ſo widely " different; or when you were ſo in- " clined to put an unkind conſtruction " on my ſentiments when in the flow of " an open temper I gave them lan- " guage to you, whom I conſider as my " ſecond ſelf."

" Good God! you make the matter " quite ſerious," ſaid Mr. Conway.

" You have, indeed, given me a " wound," replied Matilda; " and I " have not diſſimulation enough to hide " it."

So ſaying, the tears ſpringing to her eyes, ſhe walked haſtily out of the

room,

room. Conway would have endeavoured to have detained her, but as ſhe quitted the parlour, Lady Gaythorne, who had been walking in the garden, paſſed by the window, and in a moment came into the houſe, and entered to him immediately.

CHAP. XVII.

LADY Gaythorne had juſt parted from Needham, who had been inquiring with great anxiety if her ladyſhip was better.

" I am better, Mr. Needham," replied ſhe, " though not quite recovered " —but for Heaven's ſake, did you get " out of that houſe before part of it fell " upon you?—for I am ſure I expected " ſuch an accident every moment to " take place:—how can the people exiſt " with ſuch eternal riots about their " ears?"

We

" We got away by good fortune," replied he, "with unbroken bones ;—but " it called for all our fortitude to endure " the diſagreeable ſcene after your lady" ſhip went."

" Lord, Mr. Needham, what could I " have done ?"

Needham knew that there is nothing recommends us ſo much to a perſon bent upon any particular ſcheme, as judiciouſly inſinuating that the end they wiſh for is likely to be obtained, and he inſtantly replied ;

" I believe there were thoſe in com" pany who could not feel any thing " diſagreeable while your ladyſhip was " preſent."

"I muſt bow to you, Mr. Needham,
"for that compliment; for I muſt con-
"clude you mean yourſelf: for Sir
"Harry, you know, has been married
"an age; and Mr. Conway is ſtill in
"love with his wife."

"Is he?" ſaid Needham, with a ſig-
nificant look.

"Yes, indeed," replied ſhe, "Sir
"Harry told me ſo; and I am ſure I
"think ſhe is a pretty kind of a woman,
"and very amiable."

"Yes, but neither goodneſs nor beau-
"ty," replied Needham, "are load-
"ſtones able to fix the excentric affec-
"tions of men educated in ſuch prin-
"ciples as are the youth of our days;
"and

"and living amidſt the ſeductive ex-
"amples of a licentious age."

He had time to add no more, for juſt then they were joined by Sir Harry; but he had ſaid enough to give a ground for the imagination of Lady Gaythorne to paint upon, and to inflate her vanity.

On Sir Harry telling her the evening air was too cold for her to remain out of doors, ſhe returned to the houſe, and entered it, as we have before related, juſt as Matilda quitted the parlour.

Conway approached, and with that ſoft air of politeneſs which was peculiar to himſelf, aſked if ſhe had intirely got the better of her hurry of ſpirits.

"Tolerbly

"Tolerably recovered, I thank you," ſaid ſhe, throwing herſelf upon a ſeat; "but was not that Mrs. Conway I ſaw "as I came in with her handkerchief "at her eyes? Is ſhe unwell, or any of "the family? She has very weak ſpi-"rits, has ſhe not? for I very often ſee "her look melancholy."

"Of late, I think ſhe has," replied Conway.

"I hope ſhe has no particular reaſon," ſaid Lady Gaythorne.

"I think not," ſaid Conway; "ſhe is "an amiable creature; but we are all of "us apt to be a little low ſpirited, and "to have imaginary ills ſometimes."

"I am

" I am ſure," returned her ladyſhip, " it is impoſſible ſhe can fancy any thing " to give her a moment's uneaſineſs re- " ſpecting you; for I think of all the " people I have ever ſeen, you are the " moſt indulgent huſband."—Conway bowed.

" Your ladyſhip does me too much " honour; I pretend not to a faultleſs " temper."

" Oh, then it was with you ſhe was " diſpleaſed? Was it? Sure that muſt " be an imaginary grievance?"

" No, indeed; it is moſt probable I " was in the wrong."

" How

"How generous is that—ſo then, I "find even you who marry for love have "diſagreements ſometimes—and is Mrs. "Conway equally liberal? Would ſhe "vindicate you, and blame her own "conduct to a third perſon, were ſhe "led to ſay any thing on the ſubject?"

"Yes, if on recollection ſhe thought "ſhe had been in the leaſt degree to "blame, I think ſhe would; of this "I am certain, ſhe would never com-"plain of my conduct."

"Never complain!" reiterated Lady Gaythorne; "Lord I think it is a great "relief to complain—I hardly think ſhe "or any woman would deny herſelf the "relief of complaining, if ſhe had an

"idea

" idea the perfon to whom fhe fpoke
" had underftanding and prudence."

" I do believe Matilda would fo act,
" or fhe muft have changed her nature."

"Oh! you are too nice; for my part
" I think there is nothing in it. For
" inftance, if one took it into one's
" head one's hufband did not pay the
" fame attention as ufual, I don't per-
" ceive there would be any thing wrong
" in mentioning it to a perfon whom I
" thought had a real friendfhip for me,
" and who had difcretion, as we would
" mention any other little obfervation
" we make.—So Mr. Needham faid to
" me but this minute in the garden: I
" happened to be fpeaking of you, and
" remarking how happy I thought you

" and

" and Mrs. Conway were in each other.
" He obſerved, that there was no beau-
" ty or merit, however great, that
" would fix the inconſtant heart of man
" for ever; and that he did not believe
" you were more proof againſt the
" charms of novelty than another."

" Did Needham ſay ſo?" cried he haſtily; " from what motive could he be
" led ſo to expreſs himſelf. Matilda
" could not have dropped to him any of
" theſe little expreſſions of anxiety
" which ſhe has of late hinted to me—
" It cannot be.

" Good Heavens! I'm ſure I did not
" ſay he told me Mrs. Conway ſaid any
" thing to him about the matter; it was
" only his own obſervation."

" I ſhall

"I ſhall inquire his reaſon for mak-
"ing it," ſaid Conway.

"No, for Heaven ſake, don't—what
"a thoughtleſs creature I am; I dare
"ſay he only meant it as a general re-
"mark: I pray you, Mr. Conway, not
"to mention it to him; he may think
"I told it you with an ill-natured deſign
"of making miſchief, and it was by
"one of the greateſt chances in the
"world that I remembered it. Our talk-
"ing on the ſubject brought it into my
"head."

She ſaid this with an air of earneſt-
neſs, and with that naivete which ſhe
knew well how to aſſume, and which
was her moſt impoſing artifice.

"I will

"I will not ſpeak of it," he at length replied, "as your ladyſhip ſo earneſtly "requeſts it;—but I cannot think—Ma-"tilda—perhaps—but—well, however, "we will talk no more on the ſubject."

"Nor think any more of it, will "you?" aſked ſhe, involuntarily, to appearance, laying her hand on his arm with an anxious vivacity, in the motion which was really graceful and inſinuating. It is a fact, that we never ſhow to ſo much advantage as in the preſence of thoſe whom we believe to have a prepoſſeſſion in our favour, eſpecially if to this conſciouſneſs is added the deſire of pleaſing: the heart is then dilated, the features are illumined by good humour, the whole figure is unembarraſſed, and in readineſs to aſſiſt by the

charms

charms of graceful motion, the eloquence of the tongue.

"But is your ladyſhip," ſaid Conway, "really of opinion that it would not be "unkind to mention the little ſtarts of "humour, the caprices, of the being "one loves above all others, to a third "perſon?"

"Perhaps I ſhould think as you do, "had my lot been like yours."

She ſaid this with an appearance of melancholy and regret, that touched the prepoſſeſſed imagination of Conway; to whom ſhe had often inſinuated that her heart had given him the preference to any one elſe.

"Good God!" ſaid he mentally, "why was not ſuch a heart fated to "chuſe its counterpart!"

I know not whether it was the effect of accident or penetration, that led Lady Gaythorne to hit upon the right method of applying to the vulnerable part of Conway's mind. The heart of Conway was one of the beſt in the world; his underſtanding was of a very ſuperior order; and his judgement of books, and the arts of deſign, ſhewed the fineneſs of his taſte. His perſon might have ſerved as a model for a ſtatuary or painter; but though his manners were highly poliſhed and full of delicacy, there was a native dignity, and a graceful ſimplicity in the latter, that precluded the moſt diſtant idea of effeminacy.

But

But as Pope obſerves, ſpeaking of the difficulty of develloping characters by external appearances,

"Unthought of frailties cheat us in the wiſe,"

Under all theſe manly graces, there was at bottom a weakneſs, which has been generally ſtiled womaniſh, but which is certainly by no means peculiar to either ſex. Conway could not, poſſeſſing them ſo eminently, but be ſenſible of theſe gifts and accompliſhments which ſo readily conciliated to him the affection of all with whom he converſed, and which particularly recommended him to the women. He was ſomewhat too conſcious of them: a ſenſibility of heart that was ever alive to the ſoft and the beautiful, made him ſuſceptible of too high a pleaſure from the approbation of the other ſex; and though his vanity on this ſubject had not led him into actions decidedly criminal, it had often influenced him to the commiſſion of ſmaller errors, which on reflection he never thought of but with regret.

END OF THE FIRST VOLUME.

---

the very curious Obſervations of Sir W. Hamilton, on the Earthquake at Meſſina; the Subſtance of Vertot's Knights of Malta, &c. The Publiſher flatters himſelf that it will be found not only one of the moſt entertaining Books for young Perſons, but a complete Guide to the curious Traveller who intends to viſit thoſe Regions, ſo remarkable for all the Wonders of Art and Nature.

The following Collection has frequently enlivened the brilliant Circles at St. James's, Buckingham Houſe, and Windſor.

The Birth of the Roſe, the Geranium, the Paſtime of Venus, the Devil's Tail, the Kiſs of Lydia, Life's a Joke, and ſeveral other celebrated Poems are now added, which were formerly handed about only in Manuſcript.

The FESTIVAL of WIT; ſelected by G—— K——, Summer Reſident at Windſor; and carefully copied from the Common-place Book, with the Names of the Parties who introduced them to the R—— E——.

Price Three Shillings ſewed.

"This is, beyond all Compariſon, the beſt Col-
" lection of good Things we ever read; it is not a
" delicate *Morceau* for the polite Circles only, it
" muſt ſuit the Taſte of every Man who loves
" cheerful Converſation and Attic Wit.

Review for September.

FRANCE, HOLLAND, ITALY, and SWITZERLAND.

TO thoſe who make Excurſions to the Continent, the following Companions are recommended; they contain that ſort of Information which every Traveller will find neceſſary; they are but a trifling Expence, and take up very little room in the Pocket or Portmanteua.

They

They include France, Italy, Switzerland and Holland, with accurate Maps of each Country, and the lateſt Regulations relative to Travellers by Poſt, in the Diligences, by Water, or on Horſeback.

The Diſtances of the Towns and Villages from each other, and the beſt Houſes of Accommodation; with an Explanation of the different Coins, and a Deſcription of ſuch Things as are worth a Stranger's Notice, are all accurately inſerted.

The TOUR of FRANCE is Three Shillings and Sixpence.

ITALY, Four Shillings and Sixpence.
HOLLAND Three Shillings and Sixpence.
SWITZERLAND Half a Crown.

**** The above Tours may be had ſeparate.

Illuſtrated by a great Number of Plates, which include above One Thouſand Examples.

The Sixth Edition, including a Variety of Additions and Improvements, both in the Plates and Letter-preſs.

A Short and Eaſy INTRODUCTION to HERALDRY, in Two Parts.

Part I. The Uſe of Arms and Armory, Rules of Blazon and Marſhalling Coats of Armour, with engraved Tables upon a new Plan, for the Inſtruction of thoſe who wiſh to learn the Science.

Part II. A Dictionary of Heraldry, with an Alphabetical Liſt of the Terms in Engliſh, French, and Latin; alſo the different Degrees of the Nobility and Gentry of England, with Tables of Precedency.

The whole compiled from the moſt approved Authorities.

By HUGH CLARK and THOMAS WORMULL

Price Four Shillings in boards.

In

BOOKS *published by* G. Kearfley.

In Two Pocket Volumes.

The FLOWERS of MODERN TRAVELS. Being elegant, entertaining, and inftructive Extracts, felected from the Works of the moft celebrated Travellers; fuch as, Lord Lyttleton, Sir W. Hamilton, Baron de Tott, Dr. Johnfon, Dr. Moore, Dr. Troil, Addifon, Brydone, Coxe, Wraxall, Savary, Topham, Sherlock, Douglas, Lady M. W. Montague, &c. intended chiefly for young People of both Sexes.

By the Rev. JOHN ADAMS, A. M.

Delectando, pariterque monendo. Hor.

Travels are the moft inftructive School of Man.

SAVARY.

Here you may range the world from pole to pole,
Increafe your knowledge, and delight your foul;
Travel all nations, and inform your fenfe,
With eafe and fafety, at a fmall expence.

ANON.

Price Six Shillings fewed.

The FLOWERS of ANCIENT and MODERN HISTORY.

Comprehending, on a new Plan, the moft remarkable and interefting Events, as well as Characters of Antiquity; defigned for the Improvement and Entertainment of Youth.

By the Rev. JOHN ADAMS, A. M.

Omne tulit punctum, qui mifcuit utile dulci. Hor.

Two Volumes, Price Seven Shillings bound.

Either Volume may be had feparate.

RECREATION for YOUTH.

An ufeful and entertaining EPITOME of GEOGRAPHY and BIOGRAPHY.

The firft Part comprifing a general View of the feveral Empires, Kingdoms, Republics, States, remarkable

markable Iflands, Mountains, Seas, Rivers, and Lakes, with their Situation, Extent, Capitals, Population, Produce, Arts, Religion, and Commerce. Including the Difcoveries of Captain Cook and others.

The fecond Part including the LIVES of the moft eminent MEN who have flourifhed in Great Britain and its Dependencies.

By JOHN PATERSON SERVICE.

Price Three Shillings and Sixpence bound.

ELEGANT ORATIONS, Ancient and Modern, for the Ufe of Schools, originally compiled for his own Pupils;

By the Rev. J. MOSSOP, A. M.

Mafter of the Boarding School at Brighthelmftone.

"*Patriæ fit idoneus.*" JUVENAL.

Price Three Shillings and Sixpence bound.

The FOURTH EDITION, much enlarged.

(Ornamented with a confiderable Number of new Plates, containing feveral Views in the newly difcovered Iflands, fundry Animals, an exact Reprefentation of an Human Sacrifice, Captain Cook's Head from Pingo's Medal, and a Chart of the new Difcoveries with the Tracks of the Ships)

In Two Volumes,

An accurate ABIDGEMENT of CAPTAIN COOK's VOYAGE round the WORLD; containing a faithful Account of all the Difcoveries, with the Tranfactions at each Place, a Defcription of the Inhabitants with their Manners and Cuftoms, a full Detail of the Circumftances relative to Capt. Cook's Death, and an Account of his Life by Capt. King.

Thofe who fuperintend the Education of Youth of

of either Sex cannot put into their Hands a more acceptable Work, for the Amuſement of leiſure Hours, than theſe late Voyages of Diſcovery, which abound with Matter highly intereſting and entertaining.

Price Eight Shillings in boards.

Ornamented with Plates, and improved by a conſiderable Number of the moſt admired Scenes in Othello, Romeo and Juliet, Lear, Julius Cæſar, Macbeth, Timon of Athens, Henry the Fourth, Fifth, Sixth, and Eighth, Richard the Third, Hamlet, &c. &c. which was never attempted in any former Selection of this great Bard.

With his LIFE, and a Medallion of his Profile and GARRICK's, in Shade,

The BEAUTIES of SHAKESPEARE,

Alphabetically digeſted, with a copious Index.

Price Three Shillings ſewed.

Alſo, a new Edition, being the SEVENTH, of The BEAUTIES of Dr. SAMUEL JOHNSON, Conſiſting of Maxims and Obſervations, Moral, Critical and Miſcellaneous. To which are now added, BIOGRAPHICAL ANECDOTES, ſelected from the late Productions of Mrs. Piozzi, Mr. Boſwell, and other authentic Teſtimonies.

This Edition is embelliſhed with an Etching of the Head of Dr. Johnſon, taken from the Life about two Months before his laſt Illneſs.

Price only Two Shillings and Sixpence ſewed.

With five new Plates, from the Deſigns of Mr. Nixon.

The Tenth Edition of that pleaſing Selection,

The BEAUTIES of STERNE.

Calculated for the Heart of Senſibility.

This Volume contains a Selection of Mr. Sterne's Familiar Letters, the Story of Le Fevre and Uncle Toby,

FINIS.

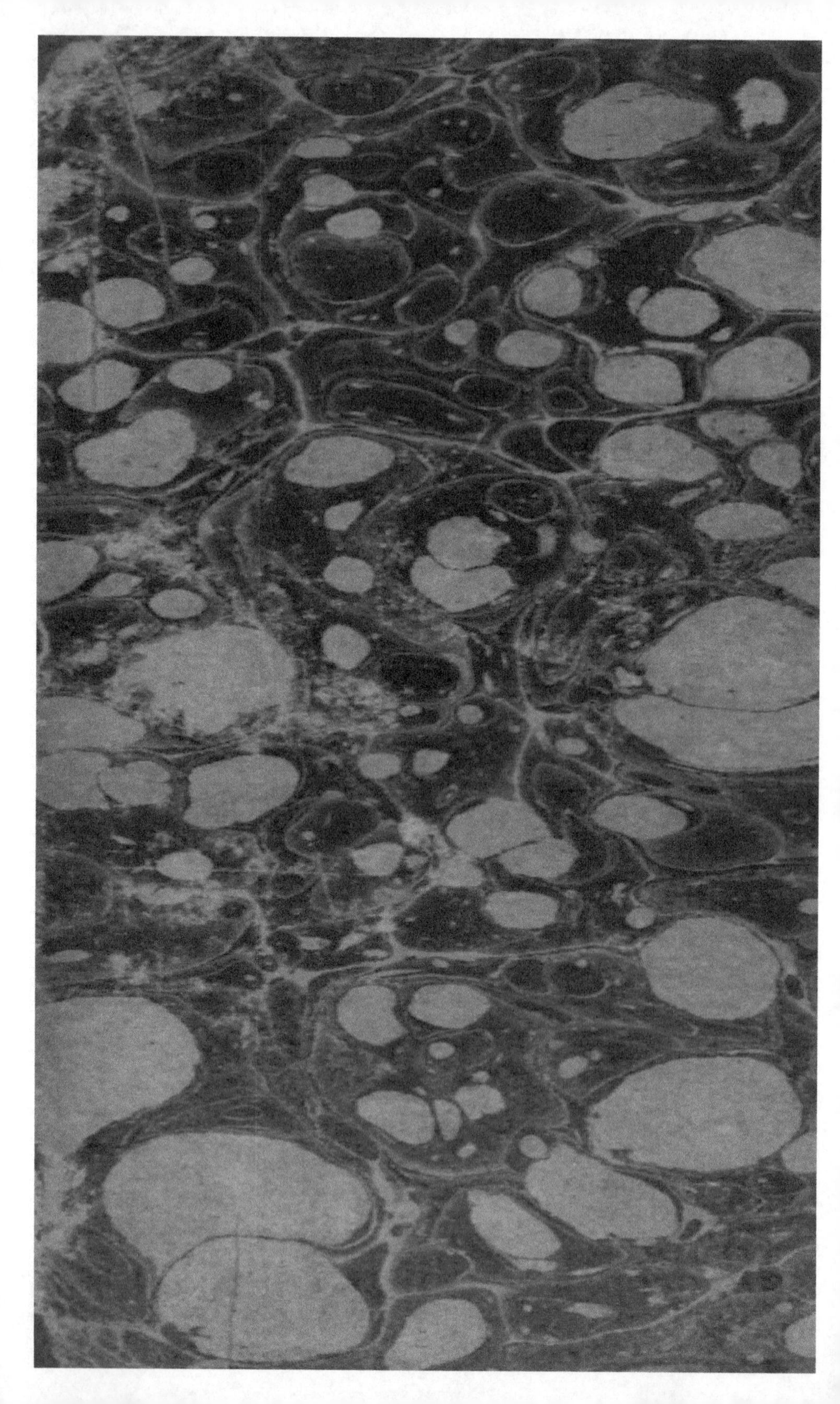

CPSIA information can be obtained
at www.ICGtesting.com
Printed in the USA
BVHW041803220819
556561BV00022B/5177/P